Adv

The Words of Her Mouth

"*The Words of Her Mouth* is a solitary beauty, presenting a vast collection of poetic truths from women psalmists. The words are radiant and diversely perceptive, touching, evoking, and moving the soul and reviving the mind. Meditate and share these verses that will strengthen your journey of faith."

— The Rev. Dr. Grace Ji-Sun Kim
Associate Professor of Theology, Earlham School of Religion
Intersectional Theology, Healing Our Broken Humanity and *Embracing the Other*

"*The Words of Her Mouth* is a beautifully written, sacred refuge. It is a powerful, compelling, ecclesiastical devotional written by demonstrably wise women. It expands ancient spiritual wisdom with current day concerns. I highly recommend The Words of Her Mouth because it presents a compelling case that God is still speaking."

— The Rev. Dr. Yvette Flunder
Presiding Bishop, The Fellowship of Affirming Ministries
Where the Edge Gathers: A Theology of Homiletic and Radical Inclusion

"*The Words of Her Mouth* is a new psalter for a new age and, like the canonical psalter, its poetry arcs forward into [a] world in which the inspiration for its creation will pass but its power endures as praying words, healing words and, when necessary, fighting words. Rev. Spong and her collaborators and co-conspirators have gifted us with this volume that gives voice to the psalms inside them, inviting us to listen and to craft our own when the Spirit rises in our throats and through our fingers."

— The Rev. Dr. Wil Gafney
Professor of Hebrew Bible, Brite Divinity School
Womanist Midrash: A Reintroduction to the Women of the Torah and the Throne

Advance praise for
The Words of Her Mouth (cont'd)

"*The Words of Her Mouth* contains compelling and truth-telling words that embody the poetic ethos and pathos of the ancient writers. With a directness that cuts through the noise, these women psalmists offer us "heck yes" moments that resonant deeply with our experiences in this wondrous and horrifying world we inhabit. I will use this book in so many ways for devotional journaling, small group discussion prompts, aids for teaching about liberating theology and the psalm poem form, as well as those personal times of lying awake simply wondering how to make it through the next day. Do yourself a favor, reader. Get it, open it to any page, be inspired."

— The Rev. Dr. Marcia McFee
Creator and Visionary of the Worship Design Studio
*Think Like a Filmmaker: Sensory-Rich Worship
Design for Unforgettable Messages*

"[These] psalms are sighs that were once too deep for words finally expressed, articulated, and announced. Longings, questions and epiphanies are eloquent invitations for deep communion. This is a book many of us have been waiting for."

— The Rev. Dr. Bishop Karen Oliveto
First openly LGBTQ bishop of The United Methodist Church
*Together at the Table: Diversity Without Division
in the United Methodist Church*

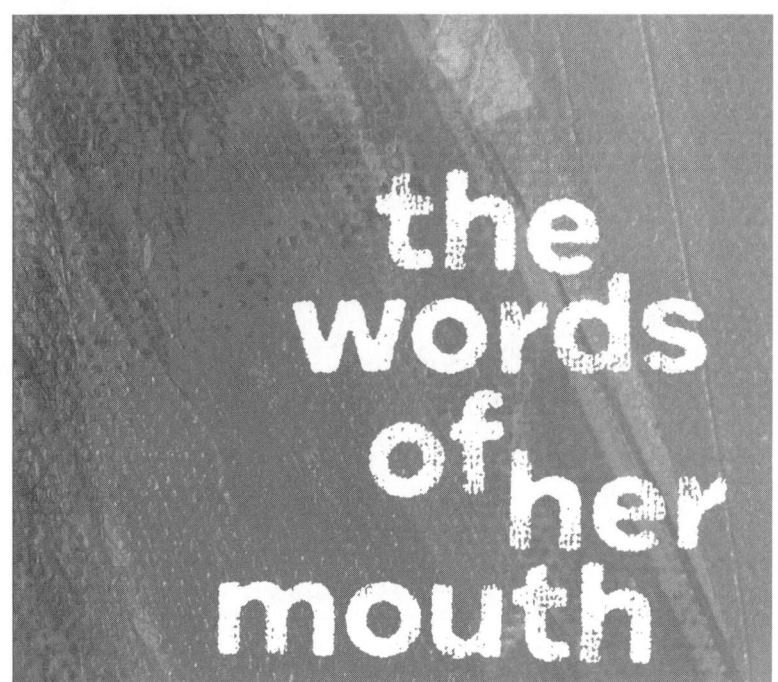

the words of her mouth

PSALMS FOR THE STRUGGLE

Edited by
Martha Spong

the pilgrim press
since 1640

The Pilgrim Press, 700 Prospect Avenue East
Cleveland, Ohio 44115-1100
thepilgrimpress.com

© 2020 Martha Spong

All right reserved. No part of this book may be used or reproduced in any manner whatsoever without written permission.

Published 2020.

Scripture quotations, unless otherwise noted, are from the New Revised Standard Version of the Bible, © 1989 by the Division of Christian Education of the National Council of the Churches of Christ in the United States of America, and are used by permission. Changes have been made for inclusivity. Printed on acid-free paper.

Printed on acid-free paper.

20 21 22 23 24   5 4 3 2 1

Library of Congress Cataloging-in-Publication Data on file
LCCN: 2019955910

ISBN 978-0-8298-2024-9 (alk . paper); ISBN 978-0-8298-2054-6 (ebook)

Printed in the United States of America

*Let the words of my mouth and
the meditation of my heart
be acceptable to you,
O LORD, my rock and my redeemer.*

—Psalm 19:14

Contents

Foreword | *xi*

1. Check In
2. Alongside
3. The Voice That Murmurs
4. I Go to My Room
5. The Acrid Aroma of One-Sided Stories
6. For Mr. J
7. Do I Have To?
8. What about the Children?
9. The Same Book
10. Tell Me Something Better
11. Like a Bird
12. Help
13. Grief
14. Eaten up
15. A Family Story
16. I Lean on the One
17. That Good Rest
18. Delight
19. Ordinary and Astounding
20. Desire
21. Thanks on Our Lips
22. Steady Stream
23. Are You?
24. Illegitimate Kings
25. What I Need
26. Her Table
27. Hope for the Here and Now
28. Give Thanks
29. The Voice
30. Favor Ain't Fair
31. A Silence from Boasting
32. Secret
33. A Newborn Song
34. Bubbles
35. Shout for Joy

36	David
37	Worst-Case Scenario
38	Exiled
39	You Call This Love?
40	Ink Prayer
41	Do You?
42	Thirsting
43	Disquieted
44	Dr. Weems
45	Not Fully Human to You
46	Imagine
47	I Want a Different God
48	Courage
49	And Where Are You?
50	The Intangibles
51	Sorry
52	Break You Down
53	Who Will Save?
54	Conversation Partner
55	Betrayal
56	Counting Tears
57	Your Wings
58	The Last Word
59	At the Expense of Another
60	Groundhog Day
61	Heritage
62	Small
63	Wee Hours
64	Not Accidental
65	Her Masterpieces
66	God of the Soft Whisper
67	The Most Basic Blessing
68	Provided
69	Semi-Colon
70	But Let Me Smile
71	Shout
72	Where Are You?
73	The So-Called Upright
74	Shall I Continue?
75	What Falls with Us?

76	Your Works All Praise You
77	Your Silence
78	Wrath
79	We Are Not Repentant
80	The People Protest
81	Bee
82	Today I Will Rise Up
83	Naming
84	Forever Home
85	To Burn with Rage
86	Turn Up
87	Would That There Were
88	My Body, Your Image
89	The Story of My Life
90	Making Trouble
91	Never Answered
92	Choose Me
93	Lolita
94	Speak to Me of Goodness
95	God of the Water
96	There Is No One Like Our Mother
97	Stars
98	Make Noise!
99	Make Yourself Useful
100	Thousands and Thousands
101	Pull Me Back
102	Wardrobe Malfunctions
103	Blessings
104	An Instrument of Praise
105	Promises
106	How Can I Confess for My Nation?
107	Hard Hope
108	Awake!
109	Swallowed
110	Wait. What?
111	Covenant
112	Remembered Forever
113	For the Mothers of Fading Fires
114	A Place to Rest
115	Circles

116	I'm Gonna Speak
117	Praise, Even If
118	Simply
119	I Will Watch for You
120	Lies
121	Created
122	A Stranger Peace
123	Tight
124	We Would Not Have Made It
125	Uncertain
126	You Owe Me More Meaning
127	Reclaiming My Time
128	Flourish the Results
129	I Was Not
130	Sophia
131	Nursing
132	Where God Lives
133	The Taste in My Mouth
134	Splay Your Fingers Wide
135	Why Did You Choose Violence?
136	Gratitude for Their Wonders
137	Too Far
138	My Work
139	I Am All These Things
140	Be a Fence
141	The Good Hurt
142	Hiding Out
143	Thirst
144	Quickly
145	The Glory of Your Kin-dom
146	Will All Crumble
147	Not True
148	Get Excited!
149	Good Music
150	Exhale Glory

Acknowledgments | *165*
About the Editor | *167*
Contributors | *169*

Foreword

The words of the biblical psalms, in phrases and whole thoughts, reside in my head and resound in my heart.

I heard them as a child, read in the King James Version in Southern Baptist worship:

> *I was glad when they said unto me,*
> *Let us go into the house of the LORD.*
> —Psalm 122:1

I learned to read them myself in the Revised Standard Version Bible the Presbyterians gave me in third grade:

> *Serve the LORD with gladness!*
> *Come into his presence with singing!*
> —Psalm 100:2

I paged through the Good News version as a teenager at Young Life:

> *I know that your goodness and love will be with me all my life;*
> *and your house will be my home as long as I live.*
> —Psalm 23:6

I studied the footnotes of the New Revised Standard Version at seminary:

> *God is our refuge and strength,*
> *a very present help in trouble.*
> —Psalm 46:1

And as a 50-something United Church of Christ pastor, I began writing my own psalms in the margins of a Common English Bible. I appreciated, I elaborated, I objected—with fervor.

The psalms are testimonies from the ancient faithful, speaking to us across time and beyond time. Yet they also remain firmly in their own context, naming the particular struggles of a community and its

Foreword

ancestors, its losses and battles and conflicts with God. As I composed and complained in the margins of my Bible, I wondered what women writers might have to say in conversation with the psalms in this season of child separation and climate change and #MeToo and #BlackLivesMatter. I invited nine women in ministry whose faith and writing I value to join me in discovering what the psalms say to us and what psalms are inside us.

We are Millennials, Gen Xers, and Boomers. We live in cities, suburbs, small towns, and college towns. We have grown up in the church and migrated from one tradition to another. We are brown and black and white. We are straight and LGBTQ+. We have responded to the call of God on our lives, personally and vocationally, even when others have questioned how we think, and what we do, and who we love.

We are psalmists now, the ten of us. In this book, we call out, talk back to, and come alongside the biblical psalms. We wrestle with patriarchy and white supremacy in our historic faith and the world today. You might use this book in a coffee shop discussion group or Sunday School class, as a daily devotional or contemplative writing prompt, and as a roadmap through the psalms or a field guide for the life of faith. May the words of our mouths be your companions in the struggle.

— **MARTHA SPONG, EDITOR**

The Words of Her Mouth

Check In

For the LORD watches over the way of the righteous,
but the way of the wicked will perish.

—Psalm 1:6

Compassionate Lord,
I just wanted to check in with you on the schedule for the wicked
    perishing.
Your timing is excellent, as always; I do not doubt it.

Yet I see a lot of wickedness and very little perishing.
There is so much suffering, division, and pain all around;
    hope doesn't exactly flourish
      in this rocky ground.
I have meditated on your laws and reflected on your words.
I am trying to love,
    trying to see the best in others,
    trying to do what is right in your eyes.
It sure would be easier to do all those things
if the chaff were blown away (as promised).

I do have one concern:
what if your patience and mercy turn out to be necessary for me?
I hate to think it, but it may be that my deeds are chaff to someone.
    In which case, please carry on.
    I'll see myself out.
And I will remember my own flourishing due to your mercy.

—JULIA SEYMOUR

Alongside

Happy are all who take refuge in God.

—Psalm 2:12

What does it mean to find sacred refuge in this hour,
    in a time when the winds of toxic change
        whirl all around me, around us?
God, I wish I felt you were laughing at the folly of those
    who seek to do harm but instead
I feel you are weeping alongside me
    as those who are self-serving and exploitative
make gains in this world,
    using the labor and necks of those they oppress
    as their footholds.
I consider what reprieve from this could be.
I meditate and reflect on the kin-dom that you call us into:
the kin-dom that affirms and acknowledges with knowing glances,
    massages the places rendered taut and tender.
    shares what it has to make sure none of us go without,
    and works to extend presence in imaginative ways
    so that we know we are never truly alone.
When I think about what it means to take sacred refuge in this hour,
    I think of us.
I think of the place where God meets me and I meet others;
I think of the ways breathing becomes easier because my burdens
    (and my resistance to them)
    aren't borne alone.
Blessed are all who take refuge in the dwelling places we cultivate to
    help each other rest,
and blessed are the spaces and moments we inhabit together.

—**ALICIA T. CROSBY**

The Voice That Murmurs

I lie down and sleep; I wake again, for the LORD sustains me.
—Psalm 3:5

Lying down, which sounds like the easy part,
is actually the hard part as it turns out.

I load this morning's dishes into the machine, I move laundry from
        one machine to another, I look at the clock, I tidy the living
        room, I brush my teeth, I look at the clock, I have to read
        what he's tweeting now, I fire off a few angry syllables of my
        own, I swallow a pill, I trip over the shoes in the hallway,
        I look at the clock.

I lie down. I roll over. I kick the blankets off. I pull the blankets up. I
        throw the blankets off. I stand up. I lie down. I could get up
        again. Toss again or turn again.

Or I could try this:
listen for the Voice that murmurs, "Close your I's."

And then
        like the dawn light that broke slowly this morning
        like the salty tide that covers the rocks at midday
        like the rise and fall of the child's breath this night;
        just like these and all gentle, inevitable blessings,
the Sustainer arrives, carrying sleep in a silver basket,
ready to offer rest as
a gift, a mercy, a benediction.

— JENNIFER GARRISON BROWNELL

I Go to My Room

When you are disturbed, do not sin.
Ponder it on your bed and be silent.

—Psalm 4:4

My mother used to send me to my room,
and I did the same with my children,
maybe just so we could all cool off.

O Mother, when I feel out of sorts with you,
and with myself,
I still go to my room

I climb onto my bed,
carrying books, journal, pens, and phone,
all the things I might reference to solve me.

But often they stay in a stack by my side,
while my mind wanders to you,
to my purpose and yours.

How else can I know?
How else can I hear you?

—**MARTHA SPONG**

The Acrid Aroma of One-Sided Stories

For there is no truth in their mouths;
their hearts are destruction;
their throats are open graves;
they flatter with their tongues.
Make them bear their guilt, O God;
let them fall by their own counsels;
because of their many transgressions cast them out,
for they have rebelled against you.

—Psalm 5:9-10

The stench of others' wrongdoing:
    the foul smell of lies and slander,
    the acrid aroma of one-sided stories,
    the putrid odor of betrayal wrapped in unmet expectations,
O God, I have an expectation that you will avenge my pain
and make those who caused it pay dearly for their actions.

But in all my pleadings, I reluctantly consider this:
    someone, somewhere has experienced me
    as their enemy, their point of pain;
    someone, somewhere has been sickened by my fallibility;
O God, someone somewhere has been on the receiving end of all
    my foul-smelling-ness
and might be praying this same prayer too.

— KENTINA WASHINGTON-LEAPHEART

6

For Mr. J

In death there is no remembrance of you.

—Psalm 6:5

"This is it!" Mr. J told me, "This is the *one*."
He held up the book in his shaking hands, eyes wild with delight.
He read aloud, "My bones are shaking with terror.
    I am weary with my moaning;
    every night I flood my bed with tears."
Mr. J made me promise to tell his story, to never forget his name.
Did *you* forget him, O Lord?
Did you deliver Mr. J?
Did you pull him out of that prison, that Black man jailed
    for some small matter, body ravaged
    by disease that came *from* that imprisonment?
Did you forget him Almighty?
Did you leave him there?
In death there is no remembrance of you.
For your sake, O God, Mr. J said
I had to remember him.
So now, here we are.
Two things I do for Mr. J:
    I tell his story, say his name,
    and I pick up my feet when I walk.
    He couldn't stand the sound of shuffling feet.
For Mr. J, I sing this psalm again.
For Mr. J, O God, you live another day.
But for how long, O Lord?

—**KATIE MULLIGAN**

Do I Have To?

Rise up, O LORD.

—Psalm 7:6

some days it's better to stay in bed
most days
to find refuge under cover of darkness
clutching indecision
wrapped in a feeble attempt
to elude the sun's rising

because some days salvation means
too much
do I have to face them
do I have to face those
do I have to face these

do I have to face the day
just because you rise

— MIHEE KIM-KORT

What about the Children?

Out of the mouths of babes and infants
you have founded a bulwark because of your foes,
to silence the enemy and the avenger.
—Psalm 8:2b

God who knows all things,

When did the bulwark become a weapon—
    silencing the cries of babes and infants
clutched to the bosom of their parent,
    holding on to their sibling's neck
        as they all seek safety and refuge?

Do you hear the choked cries of the children—
    kidnapped and terrorized,
        rounded up and locked away like animals?
Do they still matter to you?

How is it that the enemy's voice is heard above the wailing?
    The sound is disturbing;
It is loud and ugly and mean.

God, if you aren't going to do something,
    please remind us what we are made of
        and what we can do.

Because, what about the children?

— MARILYN PAGÁN-BANKS

The Same Book

Be gracious to me, O LORD.
See what I suffer from those who hate me.

—Psalm 9:13

Holy One, it seems that, lately,
the ones who hate me
are those who claim to be your people.
How is it that we read the same Book
and yet find in it such different meanings?

May I not return hate for hate.
Instead, may I offer love
and a smidgen of that graciousness you offer
to all your beloved creations.

— **BETH A. RICHARDSON**

Tell Me Something Better

Why, O LORD, do you stand far off?
Why do you hide yourself in times of trouble?
—Psalm 10:1

Daily I proclaim my faith that you are here, always.
But daily, too, I fear that you are not.

How can you sit idle, watching, as this world falls
to the ones who would destroy it before they would share it,
the ones who would destroy us all before calling us equal?

Does your gut twist like mine
       at the anguished cries of the suffering and scared?

Tell me that you hear them. Tell me that you care.
Tell me that you do not feel as helpless
       as I do in the face of all this brokenness.
Even better, tell me that feeling helpless
       doesn't mean we are.

—**LAYTON E. WILLIAMS**

Like a Bird

In the LORD I take refuge; how can you say to me,
"Flee like a bird to the mountains,
for look, the wicked bend the bow,
they have fitted their arrow to the string,
to shoot in the dark at the upright in heart."

—Psalm 11:1-2

I swipe open my phone and
tap the white bird in blue,
ready to slip away from work
to the peace of tweets about baseball,
but instead of refuge I find
a retweeted photo of a man
carrying his automatic rifle in a Starbucks,
and the story of frightened people
banging on the doors of a Broadway theatre
to escape what turns out to be a false alarm,
and here's a notification from a friend
saying her husband's office building was evacuated.

We are all on edge, hopped up on adrenaline,
some fleeing, some ready to fight.
I wonder if I would fly toward the arrow, or away?

You are our safe space, the body armor backpack for our spirits.
But what about our bodies?

— **MARTHA SPONG**

Help

Help, O LORD, for there is no longer anyone who is godly;
the faithful have disappeared from humankind.

—Psalm 12:1

Help, O Lord!
Things feel desolate and it's hard to hold onto hope.
My spirit knows that goodness and empathy still exist in the world,
      but the presence of bigots and the violence they enact is
      exhausting.
I want you to smite the wicked and strike them with terrible
      afflictions, and yet I don't want them to suffer
even though they've made it their business to make so many of us
      suffer.

So instead I ask that you strip them of the power they crave.
      Undermine their hubris.
Silence their voices until they can raise them in concert with those
      calling for healing and restoration for all.
What such restoration looks like is beyond me; I am still uncovering
      the depth of my own wounding.
It's to you—who sits outside the realm of time and who loves in the
      dynamic way that the Parent of all does—that I cry out for
      help.
Help me as I seek to help others
and work to express some measure of the love you possess for them.

—**ALICIA T. CROSBY**

Grief

*How long must I bear pain in my soul, and have
sorrow in my heart all day long?*

—Psalm 13:2a

The cycles of grief—denial, anger, bargaining, depression,
    acceptance—are idols.
They are mile markers on a highway I am not traveling.
In my pain, I am not on a clearly marked trail but bushwhacking
    through brush,
crossing unknown rivers, backtracking and circling to see the same
    spaces again and again.
These alleged compass points, meant to show progress in my journey,
are only useful if they are printed on a handkerchief;
    then I wipe my face with them and see more clearly.
I call out, and I can hear a chorus of false friends with easy platitudes,
but they don't know this terrain.
Only when I glimpse the shadows of fellow travelers on
    their own trails,
when I hear the birds and watch squirrels jump,
when the water is clean and clear and full of life,
then I remember I am not alone.
Everything is still hard,
    but I remember I am not alone.

—JULIA SEYMOUR

Eaten up

They have all gone astray, they are all alike perverse; there is no one who does good, no, not one. Have they no knowledge, all the evildoers who eat up my people as they eat bread, and do not call upon the LORD?
—Psalm 14:3-4

Sometimes they eat bread like this, the evildoers:
They drive up to a window for something called food. They eat and drive and talk on the phone and think about another thing altogether. Sometimes they eat up my people like that too, thoughtlessly, not even really paying attention.

Sometimes they eat bread like this, the evildoers:
They purchase just the freshest ingredients. The day is spent in preparation—rendering, whipping, chopping. At the end of the day, when they sit around a gleaming table with friends, the meal is filling, beautiful, delectable. Sometimes they eat up my people like that too, with care and planning.

It is hard to know which hurts more, being eaten up with offhanded carelessness or with meticulous malice.
Maybe it doesn't matter, because the end is the same.
> My people,
> o my people,
> have been
> eaten up.

—**JENNIFER GARRISON BROWNELL**

A Family Story

Those who do these things shall never be moved.
—Psalm 15:5

the first time you stepped on a plane,
it carried you across that blue expanse

and you planted yourself in a red clay soil
that did not receive you easily.

but you worked hard;
you did all the right things
you got a job
you bought a house
you joined a church;

though you heard words that carried you
back across that blue expanse,
you would not be moved.

— MIHEE KIM-KORT

16

I Lean on the One

The LORD is my chosen portion and my cup;
you hold my lot.

—Psalm 16:5

It is said that you cannot pour from an empty cup,
that you must put on your oxygen mask before putting on
    someone else's;
self-care is the key to survival and all.
When I find myself thirsty,
parched from all the world requires of me,
my throat dry from screaming against the pressure of it all,
I clamor for something to quench it.
I lean on the One with whom I can let down the high walls I must put
    up in every other area of my life.
I can silence the noise.
I can listen to my heart.
I am refilled.

— KENTINA WASHINGTON-LEAPHEART

That Good Rest

As for me, I shall behold your face in righteousness;
when I awake I shall be satisfied, beholding your likeness.
—Psalm 17:15

I find comfort in your presence, God,
        courage in knowing I come from you,
I look like you,
        I carry you in me.

My God, I can rest knowing you have my back.
        That good rest—
yaaaaasss!

The kinda rest that comes after some real good love-making,
        the kinda rest that is a full body exhale—
This! A complete release!

God, I know your love;
I know it in my bones.
        I feel known and cared for by you
No matter what hell is going on all around me,
        your light sees me through

So are you on your way yet?
I miss you.

— MARILYN PAGÁN-BANKS

Delight

God drew me out of mighty waters and brought me out into a broad place;
God delivered me, because God delighted in me.
—Psalm 18:16, 19

He/She/They delighted in me like mangoes with sticky rice and
    caramelized coconut cream:
      tasting and dreaming,
      Devouring.
They delighted in me like a good book on a lazy day:
    lost in a world of words and hopes.
They delighted in me like a sports car hugging the road, tight and low.
They delighted in me like a long-lost lover:
    fresh with excitement,
    delirious with old knowledge and passion.
They delighted in me like a good pen:
    flowing ink down the paper, thick and curly,
    like cursive writing so married to the hand that one can see
    from a glance who penned the words.
They delighted in me as if nothing had ever separated us and nothing
    ever could and stood me in a broad space, naked and strong
    and whole;
They said, "This is good, and you are beauty and love and clever and
    joy; now back into the water we go."

— KATIE MULLIGAN

Ordinary and Astounding

The heavens are telling the glory of God;
and the firmament proclaims God's handiwork.

—Psalm 19:1

There is something in the sun and stars
that makes me believe in you:
their vastness, yes, but also their steadfastness, their constant presence,
whether I can see the shape of them or not;

Something in the rising and the setting
that shows me the beautiful goodness
of dark and light, of new and old, of welcoming and letting go.

In these most ordinary, everyday realities of your creation,
made also astounding,
I am reminded that you are at work in all things—
and in me. Even in me.

Let me be a witness like the sun and stars,
an ordinary and astounding testament to Grace.

—LAYTON E. WILLIAMS

Desire

*May God grant you your heart's desire,
and fulfill all your plans.*

—Psalm 20:4

I wish God
would grant my heart's desires
and fulfill all my plans.

Or if not my desires, at least
the needs of the poor, hungry, the houseless,
those enslaved by fear or by circumstance.

If God is not a heavenly vending machine,
granting the hearts' desires of the entire world,
may the Holy One offer presence, at least:
a comforting, strengthening, healing presence for
those whose hearts are broken,
those whose lives are filled with loneliness or despair,
those whose spirits cry out for justice and shalom.

— BETH A. RICHARDSON

Thanks on Our Lips

*You have given him his heart's desire, and have
not withheld the request of his lips.*

—Psalm 21:2

And sometimes, God, we receive our heart's desire.
The job comes through. The test is negative.
The car sweeps past, without accident.
True love is found. The child grows past the difficult stage.
The ticket is a winner.
The friendship is mended. The call finally comes.
Death brings not suffering, but release.
In those moments, God, put words of thanks on our lips.
We might hold back because we are too busy with the movement of
    the world.
Why bother noticing what is right, when so much is wrong?
We might hold back because we worry about entitlement.
How can we give thanks for abundance when others lack essentials?
We might hold back because we do not wish to call attention.
If we give thanks too loudly, will you seize what's been given?
Transform our mindless busyness into focus on the world you've
    placed in our care.
Rebuke our thanklessness, God.
Use our abundance to create a world of plenty for all.
Rebuke our thanklessness, God.
Raise our voices even louder, with confidence they will be heard.
Rebuke our thanklessness, God.
Give us the will, the generosity and the courage to speak
the words of thanks you have placed on our lips.

— JENNIFER GARRISON BROWNELL

Steady Stream

My God, my God, why have you forsaken me? Why are you so far from helping me, from the words of my groaning?
—Psalm 22:1

Tears fall, steady stream,

I cry out for salvation.

No echo; silence.

—JULIA SEYMOUR

Are You?

Your rod and your staff—
they comfort me.

—Psalm 23:4b

Maybe you are my mother,
working at your sewing machine to clothe me,
picking me up at school when I have a fever,
cautioning me when I don't want you to
(but usually later I appreciate it).

You pick up when I call;
you know before I tell you,
because you know me better than I know myself,
know when it's time for a change of venue,
or companions,
reinvention, revision, or re-creation.

You are mercy and lovingkindness,
from everlasting to everlasting.

In your presence, I feel at home,
and I trust I am yours forever.

— **MARTHA SPONG**

Illegitimate Kings

*The earth is the LORD's and all that is in it,
the world, and those who live in it.*

—Psalm 24:1

Earthen clay, ebony soil, multi-hued sands—
sediments deposited on riverbanks deemed sacred
reflecting the flesh of those who bear the image of the Holy One.
Their adversaries attempt to erode inheritances for the children of the
> Divine and cast recession on the meek, stealing the blessings
> promised to them.

Illegitimate kings and false prophets spew bile rebranded as holy water.

They replace stories of our ancestors with baptized devils sitting in
> positions of influence and call it "our" history.

Earth is responding, bucking like fractured floorboards at fault-lines.
The voices of Creator's beloved grow louder, rising above the
> amplified lies of those who sought to subjugate them.

Cry out, people: speak so we can bear witness to your stories, and in
> our witness, work to restore unto you what Creator has called
> you to.
Cry out, migrants: you who traverse hard ground, sojourn through
> deserts, and brave open waters for the freedoms you seek.
Cry out, survivors: you who call attention to cultural conditions for
> abuse and leave too many bearing trauma.
Cry out, LGBTQ and SGL siblings: you who take pejoratives and
> transform them into political scaffolds.

Cry out, Native kin: you from whom this country has stolen so much, you who its occupiers continue to invisibilize when calling for justice.

Cry out, Black women: you who nurtured this nation with the stolen milk of your breasts and labor of your hands only to have it continue to demonize your children.

Cry out, you who've been marginalized.
Cry out, you who are disaffected.
Cry out, you who've been incarcerated and institutionalized.
Cry out, you who experience disenfranchisement.

You are not the problem: you are our prophets and our prophesied ones.

Let your cries resound so fully that they topple the thrones of illegitimate kings and false prophets who think the world belongs to them.
Lift up your heads! Earth is the Lord's and all that is in it;
it has been entrusted to you as children of the Most High.

— **ALICIA T. CROSBY**

What I Need

O my God, in you I trust;
do not let me be put to shame.

—Psalm 25:2

It has only been since I got "good and grown" that I have learned [how] to ask for what I need.
Maturity and a close relationship with disappointment have a way of expediting things.
I have learned the steps to the delicate have-not-because-you-ask-not dance.
My closed mouth has stood in the way of being fed;
Fear of shame has been a bigger obstacle than the ask itself.
Lord, show me that embarrassment is not the worst thing that could ever happen to me
and that there is no shame in asking boldly.
O God, help me to learn [how] to be hopeful for the "yes"
and [how] to live with the "no."
O Lord, teach me how to trust.

—KENTINA WASHINGTON-LEAPHEART

Her Table

O LORD, I love the house in which you dwell.
—Psalm 26:8

If I could be anywhere
in the world
I would always choose her table
her porch
her bed
her view.

This is not a love song—
a song about an obsession
or a crush—

maybe it should be:
a song about what love does to you
and how it makes you.

this could be a song about loyalty
and faith
and gratitude

or about how choosing love
is less like flying
and more like finally feeling the ground
beneath your feet.

— MIHEE KIM-KORT

Hope for the Here and Now

*I believe that I shall see the goodness of the LORD
in the land of the living.
Wait for the LORD; be strong, and let your heart take courage;
wait for the LORD!*

—Psalm 27:13-14

I have never been one to hang my hopes on heaven,
to see the hurts and hardships of this world
through the lens of "only temporary."
You have given this world to us and us to it
for some stretch of time, surely to be more than a waiting room.
I believe your goodness isn't merely elsewhere
but here and alive, seeking for us to know it.

Though I confess that I grow weary of
this life and place so marred with scars and fissures,
tangible and not, urgent and creeping,
I cannot quite imagine healing. Wholeness.

Still I believe in goodness—yours—alive and well, here and now.
I hang my tired hope on it.

—LAYTON E. WILLIAMS

Give Thanks

*Blessed be the LORD,
and with my song I give thanks to God.*

— Psalm 28:6-7

Blessed be, my heart sings,
for the simple things of life.
The brilliant color of the first spring flower.
The sweet taste of a strawberry.
The comforting warmth of a dog (or cat) in my lap.

Blessed be, my heart sings,
for the presence of community.
Holy moments with the brokenhearted.
Abundant casseroles for grieving families.
Presence of love in broken bread and poured cup.

Blessed be, my heart sings,
for the beauty of creation.
The orange, red, purple of a sunset.
The mountain peaks and grass-filled valleys.
The sparkling beauty of the night sky.

Blessed be, my heart sings,
With jubilant thanks to God.

— **BETH A. RICHARDSON**

The Voice

The voice of the LORD is over the waters.

—Psalm 29:3

Over the murmur of the stream,
over the crashing of the ocean,
over the shattered scatter of the rain,
over the stillness of the morning lake before the wind:
the wind, the Spirit.
Over the rushing of blood through my body,
thudding my head, breaking my heart, aching my feet:
the voice of the Lord over the waters, stirring up trouble, calling my
    name.

I hold my hands over my ears,
I play music to drown the voice,
I shut the doors and windows on the hottest day,
I crawl under the blanket and curl into myself,
and still the voice of the Lord calls over the waters,
whispering to my trembling, hidden self, a shivering lump wrapped in
    my grandmother's quilt.
They say, "Come child, let us play."

From under the quilt I worship the Lord in holy splendor.
They have given me strength!
They have blessed me with Peace!
Glory!

— KATIE MULLIGAN

Favor Ain't Fair

By your favor, O LORD, you had established me as a strong mountain; you hid your face; I was dismayed.
—Psalm 30:7

If being strong means taking a beating
        and still show up in the meeting room with a smile,
God, please don't do me any favors.

If being strong means working two jobs,
        having a side hustle,
                and still robbing Peter just to pay Paul,
God, please don't do me any favors.

If being strong means holding my shit together,
        right and tight like Spanx
                while my breathing stays shallow and my voice restricted,
my body agonizingly rigid,
God, please don't do me any favors.

If being strong means fighting
        day after day after day after day—
                with no real wins on the board—
God, please don't do me any favors.

Favor ain't fair.
Favor ain't easy.
Favor ain't for punks.

I'm tired, God.
Like you, I want to look away
      to not see, to unsee,
            to forget.
Is this even possible? How do you do it?

Want to do me a favor?
      Put me down as a "no" for the morning dance;
I am not going to make it this time

My heart is shattered.
My soul is fatigued.
My body is traumatized.

This strong mountain needs to rest. *Selah.*
      Maybe next time,
Thanks anyway!

— MARILYN PAGÁN-BANKS

A Silence from Boasting

*Let the lying lips be stilled that speak insolently against
the righteous with pride and contempt.*

—Psalm 31:18

If the divine stillness fell upon lying lips, what sounds would still be heard?
Would anyone be left to speak?
Would we finally hear the testimony of those shoved aside, talked over, whispered about?
Would we finally hear the slut-shamed, the alternately pronoun-ed, the struggling with debt, the pipelined to prison, the poisoned by drinking water, the sequestered on reservations?
If a holy hush fell on mouths that spew untruths, what stories would become known?
Might we then listen to the assaulted, the addicted, the hungry, the fearful, the grieving, the aching, the suicidal, the lamenting, the frustrated?
What sounds would die away in the wake of prevented false witness?
A silence from boasting, from false praise, from gossip, from fake news, of ranting, from false consolation, from one-upmanship, from the promises of idols.
In that enforced silence, what would we hear?
What holy stories would pour forth?
And when we are wrapped in the voice of God, in a quilt of honesty and waking witness, what will we do with what we have heard?

—JULIA SEYMOUR

Secret

When I kept silence, my body wasted away through my groaning all day long.

—Psalm 32:3

I know I can't keep it all from you,
can't keep a thing, even,
away from you,
from your awareness,
and yet sometimes
I convince myself I can.

It's like trying
to keep a secret
from myself.

—MARTHA SPONG

A Newborn Song

Sing to him a new song; play skillfully on the strings, with loud shouts.
—Psalm 33:3

The great God, Composer of the Universe, asked you for a new song and eventually a new song was produced. Others gaze at it in wonder and ask the question that has been asked of newborn things since questions began: where did it come from?

Myths abound. Perhaps it grew round and unwieldy like a cabbage. Maybe it flew in a stork's beak. The truth is stranger than any story. You conceived the new song just like you conceive anything else. There's sometimes a bit of joyful fumbling in the conception, but the process is energetic and leaves you happily, sweatily breathless.

The gestation period, following that first flush of excitement is long and uncomfortable. Sometimes there are sleepless nights, there is usually nausea. Everyone will have an opinion about what you might do to relieve the symptoms. Do not listen to them. Listen within.

The hours just before the final production are usually the most intense. Still and again, everyone will have an opinion. Still and again, do not listen to them. Stretch yourself, impossibly. Push. Breathe. Listen for the voice of the new song.

When at last it is born, hold the new song up to the light. Like all newborn things, it's not as adorable as you've been led to believe it would be. It emerges misshapen, squalling, slimy.

Do not despair. All newborn songs start this way. Its beauty will grow like the song itself grows—sometimes swiftly, sometimes slowly. Until now, you have nourished the new song.

Soon it will crawl and explore and run away from you. Soon the new song will sing itself.

—JENNIFER GARRISON BROWNELL

Bubbles

*O taste and see that the LORD is good;
happy are those who take refuge in him.*

—Psalm 34:8

I remember the first time you saw bubbles:

on a hot summer day
we stepped outside in the light,
surrounded by towering trees
a whisper of a breeze.

like a magician I pulled out a wand,
waved it in the air like a maestro;

they bounced from my hand
translucent
shimmering with blue and green, reflecting
sky and trees.

You stood enraptured,
mouth open,
like you wanted to taste them.

— MIHEE KIM-KORT

Shout for Joy

Great is the LORD, who delights in the welfare of his servant.
　　　　　　　　　　　　　　　　　—Psalm 35:27

Shout for joy and be glad!
Celebrate our triumph!
And when people ask why and question your rejoicing,
look them square in the face and tell them:
"It's because I am."

"I am" is a whole-ass statement (or the beginning of something more):
the name by which God called themselves in days of old,
and a personal state of being.
Whether whispered or exclaimed with fervor, these three letters speak
　　　volumes.

Let these words fill your mouth;
Glide over their ink with your fingers;
Listen to them on a loop;
Take them in with your eyes;
Breathe them in and out because your being is a miracle.

You are here.
You have endured.
You have made it to today—
both testament and testimony of God's lovingkindness and mercy
and of your resolve and power.

　　　　　　　　　　　　　　　— ALICIA T. CROSBY

David

To the leader. Of David, the servant of the LORD.
Transgression speaks to the wicked deep in their hearts.
—Psalm 36:1

You dare, David?
You dare?

Almighty God, tell me how you'll balance these scales
Your shepherd boy king is a rapist and a murderer; how do you choke
    down his song?
I guess with good whiskey
Because if I was you
    I'd drink
    And often
    To excess

Fucking David, always got something to say.

— **KATIE MULLIGAN**

Worst-Case Scenario

Do not fret—it leads only to evil.

—Psalm 37:8

All the women in my family carry the worry gene.
Fretting is one of our gifts of the spirit.
"Worst-case scenario" superheroes—all of us.
Need a band aid? I've got one in my bag.
Want to know the location the exit rows in the aircraft? Just ask.
Wondering about the best packing list for overseas travel? I'll send you the PDF.

And yet, and yet, and yet:
worry takes me out the present moment.
Fretting increases my fear and anxiety.
"Worst-case scenario" thinking leads me to believe it's all up to me.
If I plan well enough, I can control the outcome.

Let me turn over my worries, my fretting, my anxious planning
to the Holy One, the Creator, the Source of all.
Take away my fear, God of Love.
I am yours.

—**BETH A. RICHARDSON**

Exiled

My heart throbs, my strength fails me;
as for the light of my eyes—it also has gone from me.
My friends and companions stand aloof from my affliction,
and my neighbors stand far off.

—Psalm 38:10-11

It is said that the opposite of love is indifference.
I ache from the inside out at the distance
       of those I have called friends;
Love didn't stop the chasm of silence from cracking open between us.
Why do they treat my pain like a contagious illness?
Why have I been exiled from their embrace?
I believe with my whole heart that we have the capacity
       to be God With Skin On in our lives;
Unfortunately, I do not know how to make sense of abandonment
       by a God-bearing friend.
Or by God.

— KENTINA WASHINGTON-LEAPHEART

You Call This Love?

I am silent; I do not open my mouth,
for it is you who have done it.
Remove your stroke from me;
I am worn down by the blows of your hand.
—Psalm 39:9, 10

Somebody told me once that my mouth would get me into trouble.
They taught me to hold my tongue no matter what I was feeling
    and to never, ever, talk about "our business" outside
    the house.

I'm done staying quiet!

My silence is killing me!
It hurts worse than his fist in my gut,
    stings more than her bite on my shoulder,
    cuts deeper than their knife at my throat.

I can no longer hold back the bitter questions rising up
    like rancid bile from a place long forgotten:

Dear God, why? How could you do this to me?
You said I belong to you and that you are mine no matter what.
    So what is this bullshit? You call this love?
    Hello? God, do you hear me?

—MARILYN PAGÁN-BANKS

Ink Prayer

I waited patiently for the LORD
who inclined to me and heard my cry.
God drew me up from the desolate pit,
out of the miry bog,
and set my feet upon a rock,
making my steps secure.

　　　　　　　　　　　　—Psalm 40:1-2

I have the word "dare" tattooed on my ankle,
not because I am daring or brave or undaunted,
but because I am not.
I have spent my whole life afraid, yet compelled forward
again and again, into all the fires I fear.

My ink is an invocation.
a plea to God and Spirit, a promise that—
though fear threaten to stay my step—
I trust God will anchor my feet in the unknown to which I'm called.

Fear is ever my companion, but God is my guide:
the gentle voice calling, the outstretched hand that bids me come.
God is my daring, and so I take hold of my fear,
and together we go.

—LAYTON E. WILLIAMS

Do You?

Happy are those who consider the poor.

—Psalm 41:1a

She stands on the corner of the intersection
you drive by each morning,
each afternoon

a different sign
pink backpack and a bike
on the ground;

the poor you always have with you;
do you see them?

They see you.

— **MIHEE KIM-KORT**

Thirsting

As a deer longs for flowing streams,
so my soul longs for you, O God.

—Psalm 42:1

Does the deer let itself get as thirsty as I get for God?
Does a grazing wild animal, alert for predators, forget to drink?
Does this sister in nature become so parched that she cannot think,
    cannot work, cannot be?

The parching of my soul comes from my own failure to drink
from the fountain of all blessings.
I wander down my own path with just a few things to finish before...
    and then something else comes up...
    and after dinner, I will...
    tend to other things crowding my mind.

As I brush my teeth, I stare at my reflection with regret of what is
    undone.
My cervine sister lays down in pine boughs, quenched.
My soul rests on memory foam, desperate for a drink
    of the water of life.

—JULIA SEYMOUR

Disquieted

*Why are you cast down, O my soul,
and why are you disquieted within me?*

—Psalm 43:5a

O my soul, why are you giving up our precious energy to those who
   don't give a damn about us?

You deserve more than to be in a state of constant lamentation
because it's stopping you from really living.
I know grief feels ever-present, because what happens in this world
so easily affects your precious, tender heart.
I know what I'm about to say is going to be hard, but it's okay to lay
your burdens down,
and not just okay—it's necessary for you to be well.

Beloved, precious soul of mine:
strip down
and lay your sackcloth and ashes on the altar of God.
Wade in the waters that give you life,
and let yourself glide below as the Spirit hovers above.
Expend your energy in communion with her.
Let your movements mirror hers;
consider what it could look like to move with the freedom and peace
you experience in the presence of the Divine.

—ALICIA T. CROSBY

Dr. Weems

Why do you hide your face?

—Psalm 44:2a

In a time when I could not find you,
I turned to the words of Dr. Renita Weems,
to her words on the page of a book about your silence,
and ever since then, I recall her
when you feel absent.

I recall her and find a companion in my loneliness for you.

I don't know why you left her,
why you leave me,
why you hide yourself away.
I could blame myself—I have blamed myself—
> for not praying well enough
> or in the correct posture
> or at the proper time.

You hide your face like a mother
seeking five minutes' peace in the powder room,
but we keep looking.

Come back! I need you.

We need you.

— **MARTHA SPONG**

Not Fully Human to You

Hear, O daughter, consider and incline your ear;
forget your people and your father's house,
and the king will desire your beauty.
Since he is your lord, bow to him.

—Psalm 45:10, 11

I should not be surprised by the language
    The misogyny and paternalism should not come as a shock
but the words smack me in the face,
    reminding me of how you see me,
how you don't see us.

Womyn are not fully human to you.
    We are but objects to be acquired, controlled, traded.
Keep your promises, your riches and your nation—
    this pussy is not up for grabs.

For I know where I come from;
    I will never deny my people.
Greatness and power flow thru my veins;
    My ancestors have covered me with brilliance and magic.

I am an heir to the throne of grace.
    I belong to God.
You should bow to me...
    nah, I'm good.

— **MARILYN PAGÁN-BANKS**

Imagine

The LORD makes wars cease to the end of the earth;
God breaks the bow, and shatters the spear;
God burns the shields with fire.
"Be still, and know that I am God!"

—Psalm 46:9-10a

O, Holy One, your imagination is so much vaster than ours.
You ask us to envision it,
but we cannot imagine a world in which weapons shatter, cannot yet
      imagine a time when AK-47s are not carried into classrooms
      while fourth graders hide in closets meant for art supplies.
We cannot yet imagine a world without borders, cannot yet imagine
      a place where those who must cross those borders are not
      restrained in cages but are greeted with hospitable care.
We cannot yet imagine a world without hatred, cannot yet imagine an
      existence in which the rush of angry vitriol is more difficult to
      access than the slow necessity of love.
Enlarge our imaginations, Holy One,
that we might see the world that you have dreamed for us:
      the world in which weapons are an artifact of the past,
      the world in which borders are not merely an accepted truth,
      the world in which the harmony of love sings in every heart.
In your many strong names we pray.

— JENNIFER GARRISON BROWNELL

I Want a Different God

For the LORD, the Most High, is awesome,
a great ruler over all the earth.
God subdued peoples under us,
and nations under our feet.

—Psalm 47:2-3

I do not want a god of war.
I cannot celebrate a god who crushes and devours
and uplifts some while destroying others.

Say that it was a different time, but this time has been built
on ones that exalted violence.
We have been bleeding at the altars of such gods for too damn long.

I don't want to be the lucky survivor,
I do not want to be a favored child,
I want no favorites. I want us all to make it.

I want a better God, a gentler God,
a God of all the earth
who holds us all together and heals the cracks between us
instead of filling them with bodies.

— LAYTON E. WILLIAMS

Courage

They were astounded;
they were in panic, they took to flight;
trembling took hold of them there,
pains as of a woman in labor.

—Psalm 48:5-6

The pains of labor
are about
courage more than fear,
fierceness more than flight,
determination more than panic.

Birth-giving women are

Vessels
of the alchemy of creation;
Containers
of holy fire, forging treasures;
Midwives
of the Divine.

— BETH A. RICHARDSON

And Where Are You?

I will solve my riddle to the music of the harp.

—Psalm 49:4

In my dream I dance and move and sing and play;
I wake in the morning still cobwebbed from the dream.
I smile, stretch lazily, and put my foot to the floor—
the first pain hits my foot and runs up the back of my leg to the hip,
   the spine, the neck.

Smile fades as I rise to greet you this day, O God.
It is better if I move;
It hurts if I move.
I am already in Sheol.

And where are you, God of the mountains?
Where are you, O mighty Tetragram?
Where are you *Father* God?
Do you see, God who sees? Do you really? What do you see?

I make the coffee. Just pain.
I give praise for the painkillers and the coffee and soft slippers.
You are YHWH Jireh,
and you have provided.

Selah.

—KATIE MULLIGAN

The Intangibles

If I were hungry, I would not tell you,
for the world and all that is in it is mine.
Do I eat the flesh of bulls,
or drink the blood of goats?
Offer to God a sacrifice of thanksgiving,
and pay your vows to the Most High.

—Psalm 50:12-14

Intimacy with you is teaching me what it means to focus on the
    intangibles;
There is nothing material that I can offer you;
There is no way that I can buy your love and adoration.
This is a hard lesson to learn;
simply being me, showing up as my fullest and most vulnerable self
    has never seemed to be enough—and at the same time, has
    felt like too much.
I thought that offering things could make me lovable, could mask the
    "unworthy" parts of me;
you have shown me what delight is found in the intangibles:
the priceless value of deep gratitude,
the immeasurable wealth found in steadfast presence.
Thank you, God, for bringing me back to center.
Thank you, God, for reorienting me.

— KENTINA WASHINGTON-LEAPHEART

Sorry

Against you, you alone, have I sinned.

—Psalm 51:4a

Really, David?
    Thoughts and prayers
seeking forgiveness from God alone are not enough
        Your transgression was not simply an affront to God

What about Bathsheba?
        Where is your apology to her?
Why are there no words of remorse
       for the shame, pain and sorrow you caused this woman?
You raped her
       Then summarily sent her back home—
the stench of your semen between her legs

What about Uriah?
       Where is his apology?
You tricked him—
       created an illusion of camaraderie, brotherhood, safety.
You sat with him, broke bread with him,
       and then ordered his murder

And David, what about the child?
       The unnamed baby Bathsheba carried next to her heart?
What about your baby—
the one that became an offering for your sin?
       Where is the child's apology?

Oh David,
    King David.
You're sorry? Your confession is sorry!

— **MARILYN PAGÁN-BANKS**

Break You Down

But God will break you down forever;
he will snatch and tear you from your tent;
he will uproot you from the land of the living.
—Psalm 52:5

I almost wish that God would break you down forever,
that the Divine Parent I used to believe in would descend
        from on high,
roll up on you, and beat your trifling, repugnant ass.
You make me sick.
With casual violence,
you love evil and are repulsed by good.

Blessed is the Ancient of Days who has revealed
that your disdain for and abuse of others are rooted
        in the depth of your insecurities.
Like Legion they are many,
because it's hard to be confident when everything you've received
        has been ill-gained.

Blessed are the ancestors who abide with me,
who testify across time that the goodness of God challenges evil.
They remind me that what is at present will not always be.

— ALICIA T. CROSBY

Who Will Save?

There is no one who does good.

—Psalm 53:3

where is the good
when the innocent are
caged
discarded

and eaten up like bread?

who will save us?

— **MIHEE KIM-KORT**

Conversation Partner

Hear my prayer, O God;
give ear to the words of my mouth.

—Psalm 54:2

I wonder sometimes if I am really talking to you
or just to myself.

This running one-sided conversation between us,
the daily commentary punctuated by the occasional
desperate plea.
I save all my best lines for you. All my hardest truths.

Do you appreciate my humor?
Are you insulted by my casual tone?
Are you listening at all? Are you even there?

I never know quite what to pray for on the bad days or the good.
I'm mostly sure I'm doing it wrong.

Just let me be praying to someone.
Let me not be offering all my best lines, confiding all my worst fears,
only to myself.

— LAYTON E. WILLIAMS

Betrayal

My companion laid hands on a friend and violated a covenant with me with speech smoother than butter, but with a heart set on war; with words that were softer than oil, but in fact were drawn swords.
　　　　　　　　　　　　　　　—Psalm 55:20-21

I pray the Lord will not let me see my betrayer in the store,
because I cannot be trusted not to start a fight in aisle 7, amid the
　　　cereals and breakfast foods.

I plead that God will not let me see my false friend when I am walking
　　　down the street
since I cannot be counted on not to shove that one down into the
　　　gutter.

I beg for Divine intervention that I will not see that liar at a party,
　　　laughing and telling stories, because I cannot be relied upon
　　　to resist a teeth-loosening slap on that smug face.

The petty is high right now in my heart and I wish for
cystic acne, a bum knee, a thwarting of plans, a souring of wine, a
　　　weed-infested yard, a broken elevator, an inconvenient
　　　and permanent itch in the middle of the spine—
perhaps, Lord, all at the same time?

God, I grieve and I grieve and I grieve,
and I may someday forgive, but it's damn sure I won't forget.
The forgiveness—maybe it will be a lessening of the sting, an ability to
　　　nod in passing, a breath that fills all the space that feel airless
　　　right now.

I was stabbed, the knife twisted,
and now I carry my own insides in my hands, unable to do anything
except to be aware of the evidence and pain of the betrayal.

O God, will this pain ever end?
Will there be any justice for me?
Either you avenge me, Lord, or I know that my betrayer will travel on,
forgetting me and perhaps hurting another.
And still I wake each day, wondering if the prodigal will return.

—**JULIA SEYMOUR**

Counting Tears

You have kept count of my tossings;
put my tears in your bottle.

—Psalm 56:8

During my era of trauma recovery,
I heard that I would be healed once I had cried 10,000 tears.
I was given a small blue, hand-blown glass vase from Palestine.
Made by women, they told me. For your tears.

I don't know how many tears I shed.
But the Holy One kept count of them
and today I am beautiful, strong, flourishing.
I do not regret the wounds, the tears, or the healing.

I watch for the next woman
who might need a small blue, hand-blown glass vase for her tears.

—BETH A. RICHARDSON

Your Wings

*Be merciful to me, O God, be merciful to me,
for in you my soul takes refuge;
in the shadow of your wings I will take refuge,
until the destroying storms pass by.*

—Psalm 57:1

Your wings come in many shapes, o my God.
I name the refuges, those safe and dry places
where I have waited out the storms of life:

a polished pew suffused in yellow light,
the therapist's office with the hummingbirds just outside the window,
the solitary table where I sit now, with a cup of tea and a book,
but also:
the crowded table with many hands reaching for the common bread,
the arms of my lover, the eyes of my child,
the cathedral of trees that grow higher, it seems, than the sky,
the sun on the grassy bank of the river,
the silence of the labyrinth at dusk, walked with a few close friends
    holding candles,
the peaceable kingdom of a crowded city park on a weekend
    afternoon.

Your wings come in many shapes, o my God.
I pray for refuge, safe and dry places for all your children to wait out
    the storms of life:

Loving communities. Listening ears.
Time alone and time together. Something to eat.
The gift of loving and being loved.
A wander in creation. A way to pray.

The cacophony of diversity.
O my God, may we in our time—like you in all times—
be refuge, be wings, be a living anthem to your all-encompassing
 mercy.

— **JENNIFER GARRISON BROWNELL**

The Last Word

Do you indeed decree what is right, you gods?
Do you judge people fairly?
People will say, "Surely there is a reward for the righteous;
surely there is a God who judges on earth."

—Psalm 58:1, 11

I have never been one to seek vengeance against those who have
    wronged me.
Perhaps it's because I (loosely) believe in karma,
that cosmic boomerang from which my infallible self is not exempt.
I've never been one to believe in a God who enacts vengeance,
who is concerned with fulfilling my petty desire to have the last word—
    or deed.
Yet, if I'm honest, part of me hopes
    wishes
    prays
that the evildoers in this big, beautiful, broken world
will get what they deserve.

— KENTINA WASHINGTON-LEAPHEART

At the Expense of Another

For the cursing and lies that they utter, consume them
in wrath; consume them until they are no more.
—Psalm 59:12b-13

Turn the knife upon ourselves, for somewhere close at hand, another
    cries to the Lord for deliverance from me.
Ignorance is not innocence.
My comfort comes at the expense of another;
The satisfaction of my desires is paid by the suffering of another;
That these transactions occur with thoughtless ease does not absolve.

I hear another sing of your might.
My neighbor sings of your steadfast love
while my lips are silent.
What songs can be sung when my beloved cries out against the harm
    I have caused?
What is there to say when I am cursed with reason?
In desperation I raise my own voice in solidarity.
I amplify the complaint;
I echo the curse;
I see the pain.

I let go, I let go, I let go,
until I am no more.
It is better to be nothing
than that.

— KATIE MULLIGAN

Groundhog Day

*O grant us help against the foe,
for human help is worthless.*

—Psalm 60:11

The news cycle feels like a movie, and
we are all Bill Murray in *Groundhog Day*,
the same things happening, over and over,
a spiral of accusations and misinterpretations
from the angry, the outraged, the dastardly, and conscience-free.

Your wisdom does not elicit clicks and shares and retweets;
it does not go viral.
The ones who could bring attention to what matters do not choose to
    do so,
do not choose you.
They choose themselves.

We need the revelation that transforms lives:
care for others changes everything.

Help us, Holy One.
Our hope is only in you.

— MARTHA SPONG

Heritage

For you, O God, have heard my vows;
you have given me the heritage of those who fear your name.
— Psalm 61:5

You, O God, have blessed me
As I reflect on the ones from whom I am descended,
I offer thanks
for you have given me the heritage of those who fear your name,
those who have passed on the songs that buoy my soul.

They taught me to embrace challenge and call, saying, "Yes, Lord, yes,"
and to shift the atmosphere of a space by invoking your presence

Their wisdom taught me to ask, "Why should I feel discouraged?"
because I have the ability to take everything to God in prayer.

They instilled that you are the source of my strength,
the solid rock on which I stand,
so I know that your grace hath brought me safe thus far,
and the mercy you impart to me in this life
is a beautiful foretaste of glory divine.

When my heart is overwhelmed, I pray that you take me back—
take me back, dear Lord—
to the place where I first received you,
to that sonic womb where the gospel songs of my ancestors washed
　　　over me.
inspiring me to first believe.

May I forever hold these treasures reverently
so I can continue on in my journey,
remembering to praise God from whom all blessings flow.

— **ALICIA T. CROSBY**

Small

God alone is my rock and my salvation,
my fortress; I shall not be shaken.

— Psalm 62:6

I watch you
small
take socks and shoes off
and walk gingerly into the cold creek
newly freed
after the long winter's end:

stepping on one stone
with both feet,
pausing,
watching the creek pour water on one side,
watching the water gather on the other side;

crouching down now to
watch the fish swimming,
the insects that hover above the edge.

your shadow falls across the surface
filling their sky

safely from your rock.

— **MIHEE KIM-KORT**

Wee Hours

I think of you on my bed,
and meditate on you in the watches of the night.
—Psalm 63:6

I can't sleep. Again.
I am awake in the wee hours,
going through my list of "getting to sleep" solutions.
Turn on the Golf Channel, read a book, eat a bowl of cereal.
Meditate, listen to boring recordings, count backwards from 100.
Journal, move to the couch, breathe deeply.

Next time I cannot sleep, may I remember
the saints through the ages who awoke in the night.
May I remember that I am not alone.
May I remember, pray for, commune with
those who are awake in worry, in fear, in hunger,
those who are awake in sorrow, in loneliness, in despair.

Next time, may I remember you and
meditate on you through the hours of the night.

—BETH A. RICHARDSON

Not Accidental

Who can see us? Who can search out our crimes?
We have thought out a cunningly conceived plot.
—Psalm 64:5,6

Hear this, seekers of justice,
    and listen up, builders of the beloved community:
Evil is not accidental;
    Hate operates with intention;
White supremacy is organized,
    built into the very foundation of society as we know it,
ingrained into the very hearts and minds of those
    bred by the system,
running through the veins for whom the plot privileges.
    Every ism is its child;
Every form of oppression its descendants.

Children of God,
    we will expose the lie of white supremacy
for we were created out of love,
    called on purpose and with intent
to disrupt all hate and evil;
    for God is love
        and love will win!

— **MARILYN PAGÁN-BANKS**

Her Masterpieces

Those who live at earth's farthest bounds are awed by your signs;
you make the gateways of the morning and the evening shout for joy.
—Psalm 65:8

Morning by morning, new mercies:
the Artist of the Universe paints across a wide expansive canvas of sky;
Infinite color combinations expand, contract, fade away, disappear.
How beautiful are her masterpieces;
And then again for evensong—a double blessing!

What am I to make of this miraculous art-making,
the beauty that catches the breath in my throat,
knowing that no matter where we are in the world,
my loved one and I stare in wonder at the same sky?

— KENTINA WASHINGTON-LEAPHEART

God of the Soft Whisper

For you, O God, have tested us;
you have tried us as silver is tried.
You brought us into the net;
you laid burdens on our backs.

—Psalm 66:10-11

What God of love and mercy tests their children?
Who started that rumor?
Do they know how much damage it has done,
this idea that all the worst things in our lives are divinely ordained
 lessons,
that faithfulness means learning and bearing and rejoicing in it all?

No. I have no faith in that.

You are there in our trials and burdens,
in the fire and the flood—not as cause or twisted holy tester—
as hand holder, as co-weeper, as the soft whisper
that carries somehow across the cacophony of despair and says,

"I am here and I am not leaving.
I'm here, I'm here, I'm here."

—LAYTON E. WILLIAMS

The Most Basic Blessing

May God continue to bless us; let all the ends of the earth revere him.
—Psalm 67:7

A blessing is
a small thing, really:
a gift of relationship,
bringing depth and breadth to a communion
both mysterious and self-evident.

The most basic blessing, really:
breath, in and out,
over and over
that gives us life in this world
and welcomes us with love into the next.

—JULIA SEYMOUR

Provided

*Parent of orphans and protector of widows
is God in their holy habitation.
God gives the desolate a home to live in;
God leads out the prisoners to prosperity,
but the rebellious live in a parched land.*

—Psalm 68:5-6

When I was getting divorced and wondering where I would go
with my three little children
and my no job
and my incomplete master's degree,

I had a vision of a foursquare house.

When I went to see a rental,
it was almost the very house,
and the owner said yes
to the place that would be our waystation.

Then I believed you would provide;

I knew you would be our protection,
our four walls,
our home.

— MARTHA SPONG

Semi-Colon

I am weary with my crying; my throat is parched.
My eyes grow dim with waiting for my God.
—Psalm 69:3

God, remember that day? How I cried so hard, I thought I would never stop, cried until my voice was ragged and raw. I cried because death seemed so near and you seemed so distant.

God, remember how eventually I did stop and as my face dried and my voice returned, I wondered if maybe it was me who had grown distant, not you.

God, remember that day? How I drove downtown without an appointment and with a yearning to know that you were close, though you seemed so very far away, though death beckoned.

God, remember how I had recalled this idea of a semi-colon, even through the fog of my grief? A semi-colon tattooed on my wrist. A sign to me and others that my story was not over.[1]

God, remember how midlife seemed like a weird time to get a first tattoo, how it did not hurt as much as they said it would that day but how for weeks it scabbed and itched as it healed?

God, I remember that day whenever a stranger nods at my wrist, whenever a conversation starts with "thank you" or "me too," whenever we smile together, that stranger and I, because we've lived another day.

God, I remember. Many times every day, I look at my wrist and I remember again that death
did not win and that you are near, so near, so very near.

— **JENNIFER GARRISON BROWNELL**

1. https://projectsemicolon.com/

But Let Me Smile

Let those be put to shame and confusion who seek my life.
—Psalm 70:2a

Turn their ankles, as the blessing goes
Let me grin beyond their gaze, ever so lightly
Let me catch the eye of another who knows

Let the powerful thrash around as they do
braying like donkeys
taking up space
flailing about

Let them do the things they do because they would not listen
And save me from uttering, "I told you so"
because I do not wish to die so early
Seal. My. Lips.

But let me smile
ever so slight
and may they mistake it
for approval
Let them think me simple

Behind every closed door, in every snatched moment of peace
I lift my voice in praise to you.

— KATIE MULLIGAN

Shout

My lips will shout for joy.

—Psalm 71:23

It's not the voices that surround me on the outside
that harm me
but sometimes the ones on the inside.
I can't always hear yours—

that's why I shout.

—**MIHEE KIM-KORT**

Where Are You?

May God defend the cause of the poor of the people,
give deliverance to the needy,
and crush the oppressor.

—Psalm 72:4

Today on the news I saw a picture of a father and daughter
who drowned trying to swim the Rio Grande.
    Where are you, Holy One?
You have not defended the cause of your little ones.
    Where are you, Hero of the weak?
You have not given deliverance to those fleeing danger, poverty, war.
    Where are you, Mighty One?
You have not crushed the oppressors,
those who put children in cages,
who pull babies from nursing mothers,
who imprison your beloveds in deplorable conditions.
    Forgive us, we pray,
for these evil acts perpetrated on our behalf,
funded by our tax dollars, and
justified by our elected officials.

— BETH A. RICHARDSON

The So-Called Upright

*If I had said, "I will talk on in this way,"
I would have been untrue to the circle of your children.*

—Psalm 73:15

The children are watching.
They see what we,
    the so-called upright, are doing;
what is being left undone.

The children are waiting for us,
    the "pure in heart," to stop making excuses
to quit hiding behind respectability politics.

The children are hungry
    while we wallow in bitterness and busy-ness.
The children are dying
    while we keep score and post rants.

You say you are waiting on God?
    God is waiting on you, beloved!

Laugh in the face of your enemies!
Find joy in the struggle!
    Inspire the children to dream, again!

—**MARILYN PAGÁN-BANKS**

Shall I Continue?

Why do you hold back your hand;
why do you keep your hand in your bosom?
—Psalm 74:1

Why do you hold back your hand?
Why do you let our adversaries prosper?
Why do those who champion hate live well
    while the hustlers grinding to feed their beloveds falter?
Aren't you tired of your name being used as a battering ram
    by people who don't give a shit about righteousness or
    who, what, how you love?
Don't you hear us calling on you, for you, all across the world—
    the full measure of creation groaning in anguish,
deeply in need of relief?
What good is life everlasting if we are dying in the present
    from famine and drought, from earth's fracking pains and
rising sea levels,
    from denial of care and dignity in detention,
    bullets propelled by fragile-egoed bigots,
        carbon emissions melting ice caps,
        health insurance denials—
            shall I continue?
Do you need more reminders or supplications to turn your face
    toward your children?
Why do you hold back your hand, O God?
Why does your justice feel so far away?

—ALICIA T. CROSBY

What Falls With Us?

When the earth totters, with all its inhabitants,
it is I who keep its pillars steady.

—Psalm 75:3

I have nightmares these days, too often, about the dying of the earth:
the sun burning too hot, the oceans cut loose from the tides, and us,
screaming, burning, drowning, and it's too late, too late,
too late.

You made the earth and charged us with its care,
but we have been so careless.
And I cared, I thought, but too little, for too long.

Where you made forests, we cleared them;
Where you made mountains, we erected monuments to machine.
You gave us the vast seas, and we made a vast sea of waste.
You gave us the flora and fauna to name, and we named them:
disposable.

Will we ever learn, God? I do not know that we want to.
We will crumble to ash from the fires we set,
and your good creation with us.
The earth totters, for we have made it so.
Will you allow it to fall for our sins?

—**LAYTON E. WILLIAMS**

Your Works All Praise You

(Hymn tune "Lancashire")

But you indeed are awesome! Who can stand before you when once your anger is roused?

—Psalm 76:7

O God, your works all praise you throughout all time and space.
Creation made for goodness, with each thing in its place.
Your mercy is our homeland; your grace gives us our name.
We tremble at your power, revealed in cloud and flame.

O Lord, when you are angry, before you who can stand?
Our sin is spread before us, destruction out of hand.
We crave your intervention, the healing from above.
Come down and dwell among us, pour out your holy love.

Divine and gentle Spirit, come with us on our way.
Speak that we may all hear it, thy holy will convey.
We seek to serve and praise you in all our words and deeds.
Guide us to better living, as wheat among the weeds.

—JULIA SEYMOUR

Your Silence

I commune with my heart in the night;
I meditate and search my spirit:
"Will the LORD spurn forever, and never again be favorable?
Has God's steadfast love ceased forever?
Are their promises at an end for all time?
Has God forgotten to be gracious?
Has God in anger shut up compassion?" Selah
And I say, "It is my grief that the right hand
of the Most High has changed."
                              —Psalm 77:6-10

The pit of despair is dark, Holy One;
My body has been heaving, wracked with sobs;
    my appetite for food has diminished;
I subsist on a diet of "what ifs"
    and replayed mental tapes;
I spend my days and nights in a fog;
    rest eludes me but it hurts too much to sleep.
Sorrow's grip on my spirit is like a vice;
    the pain is visceral, like nothing I have ever felt.
My faith tells me that I should pray,
    that God will hear my call and answer;
But as yet another tear drops and I scream into my pillow in agony.
Your silence is deafening.

— KENTINA WASHINGTON-LEAPHEART

Wrath

*Often God restrained God's anger,
and did not stir up all God's wrath.*

— Psalm 78:38b

Glaciers run like rivers and trees blaze in the hills.
Do you burn it all down?
Or are we the ones who have overheated the earth?

Hurricanes wash away houses by the water.
Do you punish us with floods?
Or have we underestimated the ocean's reach?

Our ancestors blamed you, O God,
when things went to Sheol,
describing a cycle of faithlessness and retribution,
the rescue negotiated by prophets,
the return to relationship.

How many times will we be
our own worst enemies?

—MARTHA SPONG

We Are Not Repentant

Let the groans of the prisoners come before you;
according to your great power preserve those doomed to die.
—Psalm 79:11

My God, my God! What have we done?
We have murdered
We have raped
We have stolen children
We have murdered and raped stolen children
We have stolen land
We have stolen people
We have lied and betrayed and shattered whole lives
We have exterminated language and peoples

And we are not repentant.
Not really.

On the color of skin we have carved lines of inhumanity into flesh.
We have actually plagued whole peoples to death.

Let the groans of the prisoners come before you.
Shatter us, O God,
May our children's children know a better world.

— **KATIE MULLIGAN**

The People Protest

*You have fed them with the bread of tears, and
given them tears to drink in full measure.*

                                                      —Psalm 80:5

"Here are my tears," you said. "Eat.
       And these are my tears, too. Drink."

"Too salty!" we cried. "We can't eat this sorrow! We can't drink this
       suffering! We will die!"

You heard our protests, and you lifted the plate and the cup anyway.
       Most of us turned away. But some of us stayed to eat and
       drink with you, and we did not die as we had feared.

In truth, we lived. In truth, we live still.

                                          —JENNIFER GARRISON BROWNELL

Bee

Open your mouth wide and I will fill it.

—Psalm 81:10

We visited a beekeeper;
she brought out a box that held a home
a hive

and in your small, sweet hands
you held a bee.

The male bees are safe to hold, she said,
the female bees protect the hive
and do all the work;

and I laughed
at the joke

that male bees are only necessary
for procreation.

But you watched the bee
rest in your hand
safe
satisfied

you didn't even need
to taste the honey.

— **MIHEE KIM-KORT**

Today I Will Rise Up

Rise up, O God, judge the earth;
for all the nations belong to you!

—Psalm 82

Oh, the hubris!
Us good folx—
    we love to tell you what to do, God.
We forget that we, too, are part of the earth you judge
    and of the nations that belong to you.

Today I will rise up and do my part in seeking justice;
Today I will rise up and show kindness to my enemy;
Today I will rise up and spread joy and promote healing;
Today I will rise up and speak truth to power;
Today I will share love with the unlovable.

Today I am praying for judgment covered in grace
    for whosoever and everybody;

Cuz, yeah. . .we are all in this together.

— **MARILYN PAGÁN-BANKS**

Naming

*Let them be put to shame and dismayed forever;
let them perish in disgrace.*

—Psalm 83:17

There is something so empowering,
so therapeutic in the psalmist naming
exactly how she feels
about oppressors and evil-doers.

We cannot leave behind truth
even if discourse has been condensed to 280 characters.
Who has the time to listen?
Who can afford not to?

—BETH A. RICHARDSON

Forever Home

Even the sparrow finds a home, and the swallow a nest for herself, where she may lay her young, at your altars, O LORD of hosts, my Queen and my God. Happy are those who live in your house, ever singing your praise.
—Psalm 84:3-4

Yours was the first home I knew,
the first place I felt fully safe, fully stable, amidst a flurry
of different houses and custody hand-offs and family configurations
in my earliest years.

I knew my childhood church
like I knew the constellation of freckles across my own face in
      summer,
like it was part of me.
Every secret hallway shortcut, and where my name was signed in red
      marker
on the concrete under the carpet of the new Sunday school wing.
I knew that the stained-glass window in the back of the sanctuary
was the perfect width and curve to climb into from the balcony,
and rest and hide and pray.

I knew the church didn't belong to me, but I belonged to it,
and both of us, to you.
I have never been able to unlearn that truth though many have tried
      to teach me
that the church is no place for queer kids like me.

I know better.
I learned the truth too early, too fully, to ever truly buy their lie.
You're still the love I come home to.

— **LAYTON E. WILLIAMS**

To Burn with Rage

You withdrew all your wrath; you turned from your hot anger.
                                                    —Psalm 85:3

I know what it is to burn with rage,
smoke billowing from my ears and nostrils,
white-hot fury coursing through my veins,
hands tightly balled up into fists of frustration.

I know what it is to be seething from anger (fear, sadness,
         disappointment)
and I know what it is to feel a deep desire to enact that rage
on those I have deemed guilty
of not loving me enough,
accepting me enough, healing me enough, ____ me enough;

And yet you model something different altogether,
not because you are not without anger, fear, sadness, disappointment—
I am sure your heart weeps at all of the ways your beloved creations
steal and kill and destroy and break hearts (yours and that of others)—
yet you model a different way, a turning from,
a turning towards.

I'm not there yet, Holy One,
but I am willing to learn.

— **KENTINA WASHINGTON-LEAPHEART**

Turn Up

Teach me your way, O LORD,
that I may walk in your truth;
give me an undivided heart to revere your name.
—Psalm 86:11

Teach me your way;
Reveal to me how best to care for your people
      so I can live a life that honors you and those you love.
Grant me discernment, so I can detect lies and fake news.
Make clear to me what is just
      that I may turn up, show up, and shut shit down
      in your holy name.

You alone are God,
matchless in creative, generative power.
      As your child I beseech you
to give all that I'll require to be a standard-bearer
for the divine birthright that is our collective freedom.

—ALICIA T. CROSBY

Would That There Were

Glorious things are spoken of you, O city of God.
—Psalm 87:3

What makes a city "of God"?
Does such a place, do the inhabitants of such a place,
imitate the Creator in recognizable ways?
Is no one hungry?
Does everyone have a bed?
Are those with mental illness accompanied
and those who are dying never left alone?
Does "all are welcome" have real meaning?
O God, would that there were such a city, on this earth, in our time.

— JULIA SEYMOUR

My Body, Your Image

*You have caused my companions to shun me,
you have made me a thing of horror to them.*

— Psalm 88:8

I really was a thing of horror to them, Holy Friend—
the scholarship summer camp girl, the tomboy
—so naïve someone had to tell me (after she offered a sugary
    compliment about my thrift store outfit and I smiled,
    pathetically grateful, and said "Thank you") that she was
    kidding.
My body really was a thing of horror to them, Holy Friend,
which I knew when the queen bee in her logo shirt demanded to know
    of a cabin-full of (as-yet-except-for-me unmenstruating)
    tweens "who put a used pad right in the garbage" where she
    had to see it?
Since my body was a thing of horror to them, Holy Friend,
I thought I was a thing of horror to you too.
Years later, I learned otherwise, in a circle of women made holy by
    your presence. We sat together on the crinkly, late-summer
    grass and told the story of our first blood. And some of us
    laughed, and some of cried, and all of us shook our heads and
    said we wished we'd known then what we finally know now.
We could never be a horror to You, Holy Friend.
Each of us created as we are in your
    bloody, bodacious, glorious, gorgeous image.

— JENNIFER GARRISON BROWNELL

The Story of My Life

*LORD, where is your steadfast love of old,
which by your faithfulness you swore to David?*
—Psalm 89:49

The story of my life, Lord:
every time I trust, someone hurts me;
every time I feel assured, something goes wrong;
And so I question where I stand with you.

I pray for others,
for their healing and their safety,
for their bodies, minds, and spirits,
and I believe you will be steadfast for them,
as if you love everyone,
just not me.

Maybe we all have this story:
our lives feel fleeting, fractious,
unsustainable in the ultimate.

How long, O God? How long?

— MARTHA SPONG

Making Trouble

*The days of our lives are seventy years,
or perhaps eighty, if we are strong;
even then their span is only toil and trouble...*
—Psalm 90:10

Seventy or eighty years to make trouble.
Perhaps I only have 47;
my mother was sure she'd be dead by 40
—she is now 76—
she is astounded every day.

Seventy or eighty years to cause trouble.
Lately I am sure I am dying—
preserve my life, O God!
Do you know how much trouble I could create with just three more
    years?

I promise you, Almighty Creature of Nothingness and Everything,
give me three more years and I will make you laugh,
deep belly laughter that cannot be stopped, bubbling over into the
    world.
Disrupting, confusing laughter—
I will make the Almighty chortle with glee.

Who knows what might happen at the whim of an entertained God?
Don't you want to see?
Three years more, O God,
three years.
What is that to you, anyway?

—KATIE MULLIGAN

Never Answered

When they call to me, I will answer them;
I will be with them in trouble,
I will rescue them and honor them.
With long life, I will satisfy them,
and show them my salvation.

—Psalm 91:15-16

I saw a meme today that said, "The best time to call me is text message."
Sometimes that is what prayer feels like to me, Holy One:
    a ringing phone that is never answered,
    voicemail that is always too full,
An unfulfilled promise to call back.
"Give me a call anytime if you need anything!" is what I imagine you saying,
    yet like my smartphone-addicted friends,
    it isn't actually what you mean.
I'm not quite sure how to text heaven, and even if I knew how,
are you charged enough to receive it?

— KENTINA WASHINGTON-LEAPHEART

Choose Me

In old age they still produce fruit;
they are always green and full of sap.

—Psalm 92:14

Holy One, I'm getting old.
I hear news stories about "older adults" and they are people my age.
For more than ten years, AARP has been inviting me to join them.

I am discovering the ageism that lives inside of me,
the shame and embarrassment I feel about my advancing age,
    my changing body.

And yet, Holy One, you called old ones to your service:
Abraham and Noah,
Sarah, Naomi, Anna, Elizabeth,
chosen by you for special tasks.

Choose me, God of creation.
May I know my belovedness just as I am:
serving you all my days,
producing fruit, always green, and full of sap.

— BETH A. RICHARDSON

Lolita

The floods have lifted up, O LORD,
the floods have lifted up their voice;
the floods lift up their roaring.

—Psalm 93:3

I call the waters Lolita[1]—
    they are magnificent!
Their colors reflect the sky;
    Their movement reveals joy, sometimes terror;
Their sounds speak both life and death.

Lolita shares with me the rhythm of life:
their ebbs and flows soothe me.
    I am astounded by their abundance;
Their power reminds me to take heed of my place,
    our connection.

They need love and demand protection;
They cannot be contained and are not for sale.
Lolita is not mine,
    they are not yours.
Lolita belongs to creation.
Lolita belongs to God.
    They are beloved.

— **MARILYN PAGÁN-BANKS**

1. "Lolita Lebron is an icon of the Puerto Rican Independence movement. Lolita is what I call the lake/water."

Speak to Me of Goodness

When the cares of my heart are many,
your consolations cheer my soul.

—Psalm 94:19

When the cares of my heart are many,
you speak to the core of my soul.
As my Creator you know and have formed me;
You possess the ability to address my most hidden concerns

Blessed are you who ministers to me in bathrooms and in sleeping
        hours
for you know that my mind is most at ease
with feet planted on cold, grouted tiles or in the midst of REM cycles.

Speak to me of goodness;
Declare your acknowledgment of the pain borne by my reality;
Make way for visitations with my ancestors
so we can commune with your spirit in my dreamscapes
or immersed in bathing waters.

I just pray you keep showing up to and for me
in ways that have meaning to me
and places you know hold meaning for us.

—ALICIA T. CROSBY

God of the Water

In God's hand are the depths of the earth;
the heights of the mountains are God's also.
The sea is God's who made it,
and the dry land, which God's hands have formed.
—Psalm 95:4-5

I go to the ocean a lot now.
I missed it, like a hunger, a gaping hungry hole,
all the years I was gone from this coast,
> looking for myself in

landlocked places.
My brother wonders aloud how long it will be
before I learn to take it for granted—
the ocean down the street. He hasn't been in years.

I can't imagine I ever will, even though it still scares me a little,
like it always has, its currents and riptides,
> its hungry creatures and endless depths.

But mostly it feels like God.
When I go to the water, I am certain God meets me there:
big enough to stretch across the world beyond what any eye can see,
strong enough to take whatever I carry and bear it out across the tides,
tender enough to hold me,
and close enough to roll in over my toes across the sand and say,
> "Hello love."

—LAYTON E. WILLIAMS

There Is No One Like Our Mother

(Hymn tune "Hymn To Joy")

*Ascribe to the LORD, O families of the peoples,
ascribe to the LORD glory and strength.*

— Psalm 96:7

Voices sing, "Our God is good all the time and everywhere,"
Prayers and praise and adulation in response to holy care
There is no one like our Mother, none pour forth in pow'r like her
Love that gives us life eternal, grace that makes our freedom sure.

False the idols that surround us, lies their word, untrue their claim.
Off'ring death at low, low prices, our souls' pain their only aim.
Always present, our God saves us with the truth we have a home.
Resting in the arms of mercy, anchored souls no longer roam.

Let us then reject the mistrust, fear, and hurt that fill our days.
Join we all in celebration, taking up God's work and ways.
We are fam'ly, all united by the One who loves us best.
We are called to work together, til we reach our holy rest.

— **JULIA SEYMOUR**

Stars

The heavens proclaim God's righteousness.
—Psalm 97:6

That one night in the mountains

the sky lit up
with falling stars
one after another

each one like a note
together, a song.

— MIHEE KIM-KORT

Make Noise!

Make a joyful noise to the LORD, all the earth.

— Psalm 98:4

Make a joyful noise—
not a beautiful noise or a perfect noise or a balanced noise;
It doesn't even say music.
Make *noise* all the earth!
Pound on those drums,
scream your screams,
shout into the void,
stomp your feet,
beat on the pews,
laugh and cry and holler!
Rough and tumble and loud like baby kittens and grown lions,
stampede like cattle,
bray like donkeys!
Crash to the ground like trees struck by lightning,
burn and crackle and snap and roar like fire out of control!
Make a joyful noise to the Lord all the earth!
Don't you dare be silent;
Don't you dare hold anything back!
With everything that you are, with every part of your being,
make *noise*!
Praise the Lord!

— **KATIE MULLIGAN**

Make Yourself Useful

Worship at God's footstool.

—Psalm 99:5a

I don't descend from people who kneel
or from priests in elaborate vestments,
but from Methodist ladies who wore hats and gloves
and low-heeled, genteel (not new) shoes,
who stood to sing and sat to pray.

In church, they sat up straight in their front pew,
but in the world, they unleashed themselves
for goodness' sake.

Their lives of service to you
took them into schools and clinics,
board meetings and courtrooms,
to agitate and educate.

"Make yourself useful," they told me,
"as well as decorative."
For God is great,
and God is good
and calls us to work.

—MARTHA SPONG

Thousands and Thousands

Enter God's gates with thanksgiving, and God's courts with praise.
Give thanks, bless God's name.

—Psalm 100:4

Inside Chartres Cathedral, it is cool and dark after the heat and dust
    of the outside courtyard.
A sign in many languages explains that on Resurrection Day,
the townspeople would form a ring around the labyrinth and the
    priest would
solemnly walk the path to the center, carrying
a huge yellow ball of yarn.
Still solemn, the priest and the townspeople would toss
the ball back and forth, creating a dance or a web or a wheel—
a potent symbol of Christ resurrected,
a serious expression of a serious faith.
Having read the signs, I take off my shoes and feel the cool stones
    under my toes.
I think about that solemn priest and his ball of yellow yarn
as I take one along the path that thousands of thousands of feet have
    walked.
I reach the center, grooved and worn, and I wonder,
if it was so very solemn, so very serious,
why can I hear echoes of jubilant laughter?

— JENNIFER GARRISON BROWNELL

Pull Me Back

I will walk with integrity of heart.

—Psalm 101:2

I long to walk with integrity of heart.
Truthful, honest, reliable, upright,
knowing the difference between good and evil,
following the right path.

And yet, finding the path has gotten so complicated.
I participate in global warming, the destruction of the planet,
in my daily ordinary routines.

I usually remember my reusable bags at the grocery store.
But what about the dozens of plastic bags in my pantry?
I can't convince my workplace to stop using single-use water bottles.
And now, straws! It's so hard to choose between the sea creatures
and the beverage I usually spill down the front of my shirt.

Pull me back, Holy One, towards integrity of heart,
that I might find simple ways to make a difference in the world.
And, Holy One, give me a spirit of mercy and forgiveness
For myself and for the others walking this fragile planet.

— **BETH A. RICHARDSON**

Wardrobe Malfunctions

Long ago you laid the foundation of the earth,
and the heavens are the work of your hands.
They will perish, but you endure;
they will all wear out like a garment.
You change them like clothing, and they pass away;
but you are the same, and your years have no end.

—Psalm 102:25-27

It's difficult to think of God as having wardrobe malfunctions.
Do God's buttons fall off? Do hems fall out of God's pant-legs?
> How does God decide when a "foundation garment"
> needs to be shed or upgraded to the newer model?
As I consider the wide flowing skirt of the seas,
the expansive sweater of the rolling plains,
the sturdy shoes of the mountain range,
> I am struck by how we humans are doing
> quite a poor job of tending to God's closet.

— KENTINA WASHINGTON-LEAPHEART

Blessings

Bless the LORD, O my soul,
and do not forget all his benefits.

—Psalm 103:2

Blessings
are often mixed,

disguised or confused
depending on who's looking at them
or getting them
or giving them;

They consecrate,
they anoint,
they ordain,
they glorify,

but they burden, too.

—MIHEE KIM-KORT

104

An Instrument of Praise

I will sing to the LORD as long as I live;
I will sing praise to my God while I have being.
May my meditation be pleasing to him,
for I rejoice in the LORD.

—Psalm 104:33-34

I am an instrument of praise
      Melodiously designed to worship my God
Harmoniously created to live in adoration
I cannot contain my song of thanksgiving!
      Can you hear my heart as it belts out with every beat:
      I am enough!

— MARILYN PAGÁN-BANKS

Promises

God is mindful of their covenant forever,
of the word that they commanded,
for a thousand generations.

—Psalm 105:8

God never crosses a threshold and forgets
    what was on the Divine mind.
Never, in the midst of creation, does God take a coffee break
    and then lose the thread of a project.
God's knitting closet does not contain a dozen project bags,
    waiting for completion.
The holy appointment book overflows with names, situations,
    meetings, encounters, and plans—
    all equally important and beloved.
God acknowledges mentions and tags; God never fails
    to read and respond to their private messages.
It goes without saying that God notices
    name-dropping and doesn't give any extra attention.
Even when God's desk is cluttered, no wedding, funeral, or
    mud pie tea party goes unattended by holy presence.
If God had a typical human body,
    the pinky finger would be out-sized, noticeably so,
    revealing all the promises kept
    from generation to generation.

—JULIA SEYMOUR

How Can I Confess for My Nation?

*Both we and our ancestors have sinned;
we have committed iniquity, have done wickedly.*
—Psalm 106:6

How can I confess for my nation?
God, I'm asking because I really don't know,
I don't have a ton of positive regard for it at present,
and my confession is actually a complaint
> because the list of sins it commits against you and me
> and my beloved are the same.

Descend from your holy place and do something.
My ethical commitments stop me from praying violence on people,
so maybe use enough sacred force to get the atrocities to stop;
Redistribute resources stored by those who've harmed us
> for the sake of our healing;

Take what was ill-gained by our oppressors and give it (back) to the
> people.

May those possessing wisdom and strategy become known to you
so we can create restorative systems of provision so none of us ever
> experiences lack again.

Deliver us from the oligarchs who manipulate laws, economies, and
> policies for the sake of their profit.

Give to us prophets who will bring hidden horrors to our
> consciousness,

who cast vision for a better way of being,
so that when we pursue liberation
our freedom-seeking is communal and complete.

— **ALICIA T. CROSBY**

Hard Hope

O give thanks to the LORD, for God is good;
for God's steadfast love endures for ever.
Let the redeemed of the LORD say so,
those God redeemed from trouble
and gathered in from the lands,
from the east and from the west,
from the north and from the south.
—Psalm 107:1-3

It's harder than it used to be for me to imagine all of us gathering,
a drawing together from the far-off edges of the world.
These days it feels so much more like a scattering, a shattering,
a graveyard of broken relationships and walls built to keep us apart.
"What God has joined together in love let no one tear asunder."
We are trying so hard.

It's harder than it used to be to imagine redemption, a world made
      better,
a humanity unfettered by brokenness, bigotry, fear, and despair.
It's harder than it used to be to believe that you're there.
But it's easier to believe that I'm wrong—we are so often wrong.

Please let me be wrong.

—**LAYTON E. WILLIAMS**

108

Awake!

Awake, my soul! Awake, O harp and lyre! I will awake the dawn.
—Psalm 108:1b-2

My tools will not be shovels or data.
My tools will not be guns or money.
My tools will not be backhoes or computers.
My tools will be a harp and a lyre.
And with these tools, I will make this song.
I will take this song into the street.
It's loud in the street; somewhere a car alarm is sounding.
My neighbor on this side has her television turned all the way up again;
I hear somebody blow something up before a commercial
interrupts to sell a pill that relieves anxiety.
My neighbor on that side is using his cursed leaf blower again,
although he just did that yesterday.
What does he have against leaves anyway?
The song begins so softly at first that I almost despair.
Then slowly, louder reverberations build.
Louder still, and this song will become a shout, a whoop, a holler.
Louder than anything any tool has made before: louder than
car alarms and televisions and even (a curse be upon them) leaf
      blowers.
This song will be louder, even, than my own loudest thoughts.
This song will wake me up.
This song will wake us all up.

—JENNIFER GARRISON BROWNELL

Swallowed

I am gone like a shadow at evening.

—Psalm 109:23

I am nothing and nobody and I do not matter here
and may that be a blessing unto me, O God,
for out of curses you make blessing.
I praise you on my worst of days for all it means
      is that you are close—
      as close as my breath
      as tight as my skin.
You are in me, O God;
I swallow you whole.
The evening comes and I fade;
      invisible I walk the streets
      nothing and nobody
      and isn't it better this way?
Bless the God of the night who receives my shadow into their
      wholeness.
With you, O God, I breathe to the rhythm of your night
cradled in the ambiguity of late night light;
I am nothing and nobody
a shadow swallowed by the night.

— KATIE MULLIGAN

Wait. What?

The LORD says to my lord,
"Sit at my right hand
until I make your enemies your footstool."

—Psalm 110:1

Wait. What?

Don't shatter heads for me,
even the heads I think deserve it.

Show your power otherwise.
Change them
(and me):
turn our minds toward justice;
tune our hearts for mercy;
make enemies companions
gathered around a table with you

— MARTHA SPONG

Covenant

God has commanded the covenant forever.

—Psalm 111:9

Don't promise me anything
but yourself,

even if I ask for more.

— MIHEE KIM-KORT

Remembered Forever

For the righteous will never be moved; they will be remembered forever.
　　　　　　　　　　　　　　　　　—Psalm 112:6

Blessed is she who stretches dollars and SNAP credits
to ensure that her kin and the block get fed.
May she be remembered forever.

Righteous are they who open their homes and arms
　　　to queer and trans bbs
dealing with housing insecurity after experiencing familial exclusion,
May they be remembered forever,

Holy is he who operates the mobile barber shop and runs specials
so homelessness and economic hardship aren't deterrents to folks
　　　looking and feeling fresh,
May he be remembered forever.

Anointed are all who do what they can with what they have
to celebrate and affirm the sacred worth of others;
The everyday kindness and sharing they exercise
help us imagine a tomorrow worth fighting for and living into.

If ever we forget their names, bring to our remembrance their legacies
　　　of love, O God.
Help us walk in their footsteps
and speak of them with reverence from generation to generation
so they will be remembered forever.

—ALICIA T. CROSBY

For the Mothers of Fading Fires

He gives the barren woman a home,
making her the joyous mother of children.
—Psalm 113:9a

I have never been the type
who runs toward other people's babies with open arms.
I have always been a little bit afraid of their cries,
    their snot, their tiny fragile bodies,
    and my own awkward unknowing.

And yet, when I was young I had—at any given time—
six names picked out
for the children I would have.
I didn't know then that at 33 I'd still carry names like secrets on
    the tip of my tongue
waiting for someone to give them to,
that the closest thing I'd have to a child is an aching hope in my chest,
    fading like a fire losing oxygen but somehow
    burning hotter as it goes.

I've wondered on my worst days:
Did that fear, that awkward uncertainty,
that missing instinct, at some point, render me
unworthy of motherhood?

If a baby in the arms of a barren woman is the sign
    of God's steadfast love,
what does that mean for those of us who carry our children only as
a fading fire in our chest?

—LAYTON E. WILLIAMS

A Place to Rest

Judah became God's sanctuary.

—Psalm 114:2

Holy One, may we be your sanctuary.
Just for a little while, may we give you a place to rest:
we, your people, fashioned by your hands, knit together in your womb,
we, your people, written on your heart, held in the palm of your hand,
we, your people, apple of your eye, bearers of your love.

Linger here, just for a little while and live in our spirits.
Sweep out the corners of our hearts and make a place here
that your love might shine forth into this broken world,
that we might be your face, your heart, your tender presence to those
    we meet,
that they might know you through knowing us.

Just for a little while, Holy One, may we be your sanctuary.

— BETH A. RICHARDSON

115

Circles

The heavens are the LORD's heavens, but the earth he has given to human beings.

—Psalm 115:16

Let's make a big circle.
Let's make it big enough for those we love and those we hate.
Let's make it so big that those we love prosper, and those we cannot love prosper, too.
Let's make a circle big enough and wide enough and abundant enough that scarcity and fear and hate are what is squeezed out, but not people—never, never, never God's children.
Let's make a big circle where every single created thing knows that we are one family, because in this big circle, all living beings share the same first name, and that name is Beloved.
Let's make it big enough for the stars that shine at night and the blade of grass that pokes its head up through concrete.
Let's make it big enough for creatures of the sky—the bald eagles and the crows that chase them, and the hummers at your feeder.
Let's make that circle big enough for the creatures of the sea—the whale and the salmon and the monsters down below where it is too dark and cold for life and yet somehow life thrives.
Let's make that circle big enough for grizzly bears and anacondas and termites.
Let's make that circle big enough for seal pups and kittens with big eyes and baby birds in nests, reaching for the worm which is also part of the circle.
Let's make that circle big enough for arctic ice floes and tropical banyan trees and purple mountain majesties and the sand you just found in your sneakers from last summer's trip to the beach.
Let's make a big circle.

— JENNIFER GARRISON BROWNELL

I'm Gonna Speak

Return, O my soul, to your rest,
for the Lord has dealt bountifully with you.

—Psalm 116:7

I'm gonna speak to that thing!

I'm gonna speak rest into my own weary soul.
I'm gonna speak healing into my own body.
I'm gonna speak peace into my own mind.
I'm gonna speak joy into my own heart.
I'm gonna speak purpose into my own work.
I'm gonna speak well-being into my own family.
I'm gonna speak shalom into my own community.
I'm gonna speak life into the universe.

For God has spoken love out of chaos
        and God's Word modeled for us
                the power of this very love.

I'm gonna speak to that thing—for me
        and for you
                for us.

— MARILYN PAGÁN-BANKS

117

Praise, Even If

Praise the LORD, all you nations!

—Psalm 117:1

Praise the Lord:
in whatever language you desire,
by whatever name you choose,
even if you reject lordship and see it another way.

Praise the Lord, even if nationhood is an abomination.
Praise even if
scriptures
organized religion
liturgy
litany
prayer
ritual,
yes, even if the very concept of God
is anathema to you.
Praise!
Sing!
Dance!
Create!
Be!
Praise!

— KATIE MULLIGAN

Simply

*The stone that the builders rejected
has become the chief cornerstone.*

—Psalm 118:22

Holy One, I have no interest in being in charge—
the head
most important
or the center of attention;
I simply want to be acknowledged.

—KENTINA WASHINGTON-LEAPHEART

I Will Watch for You

My eyes fail from watching for your salvation,
and for the fulfillment of your righteous promise.
—Psalm 119:123

I watch for a bend toward justice.
I remember the names:
      Sandra, Eric, Trayvon, Philando, Tamir.
I shut my heart against lies.
I put my shoulder into working for the truth.
I weep over dead grade-school students, tiny hands and feet
      playing no more.
I hate the idols that surround me,
      symbols of systems claiming power that is not theirs.
I wait for you. I wait for your intervention. I watch.
My eyes burn with alertness.
They are dry, and the oil of sweat stings the corners.
Still, I watch. I work and I watch.
Where are you?
I believe you keep your promises and yet,
and yet,
where are you?
I have pored over your written word. I have listened for your voice.
      I trust.
Where are you?
How long will this go on?
My eyes grow heavy with the watching. They want to sleep.
      They want to rest.
But if you are going to move, I don't want to miss it.
I reflect on the truths I know, the ways that bring freedom;
I search to discern what I have missed.

My prayers flicker between word and deed;
my soul is restless
    not to be ignored.
I fight, I fight, I fight, and I will not complain,
because it is a privilege to wrestle for the truth.
Did I forget a commandment? Have I failed in some way?

I watch for you, but you do not seem to come.
    My eyes are so tired.
Are you going to keep your promises?
Will there be justice?
Will healing come?
Is there enough balm in Gilead to soothe these sin-sick souls?
Maybe it is time for me to have my eyes checked,
to account for my astigmatism;
But let me keep my eyes open, my body working, my song steady.
I will watch for you.

— JULIA SEYMOUR

Lies

Deliver me, O LORD,
from lying lips,
from a deceitful tongue.

—Psalm 120:2

Accommodating.
That's a word to describe the times I've lied for safety's sake,
to shield myself,
but the same tactic works to gain an advantage—
and then it becomes something else,
artful, manipulative, deadly.

Like a bat smashing a windshield,
or the soft touch that redirects a toddler,
a lie changes things.

It's faking it for a good cause,
or acting like you care just to end the conversation.

Lies are clever, easy, convenient.

I cannot lie to you.

— MARTHA SPONG

Created

I lift up my eyes to the hills—
from where will my help come?
My help comes from the LORD,
who made heaven and earth.

—Psalm 121:1-2

I go to the mountains
       and I have come home to you, Holy One.
Rising up from the flat plains,
       your peaks live in the clouds.
       Snow covers you in winter and in summer.
Your rocks are dwellings for great and small.
Eagle and wren,
       bighorn sheep and chipmunk,
       aspen and columbine,
       all live in harmony under your protection.
Your streams of living water dance from the peaks to the prairies,
       singing the river song of strength and beauty,
       wearing down boulders and sustaining life.
You, Holy One, created the mountains, the skies,
       the rivers, the creatures, the forests, the grasslands.
You created all of life.
And you, Holy One, created even me.

—BETH A. RICHARDSON

A Stranger Peace

Pray for the peace of Jerusalem:
"May they prosper who love you.
Peace be within your walls,
and security within your towers."

—Psalm 122:6-7

There was a shooting on Sunday and yesterday, talks of nuclear war, and this morning at the gym the TV screens all flashed politicians spewing twisted rhetoric, and I wonder:
      Is it getting worse like it feels it is?
      Or has it always been this bad?

This weekend I will drive to my brother's house and scoop up my niece and my nephew will run over to hug me hello, their joy juxtaposed with everything else this week has shown me.
And I will wonder, as I often do:
      Will they ever know a happy world?
      Will they ever even know what peace is?

Have we ever even known what peace is?
Or is it such an utter stranger that we would pass it
on the street begging for help
and avert our eyes,
      hurrying on into the broken world,
      unwilling to spare the necessary change?

— LAYTON E. WILLIAMS

Tight

*As the eyes of a maid
to the hand of her mistress,
so our eyes look to the LORD our God,
until God has mercy upon us.*

—Psalm 123:2

With a smile stretched across her face

tight like a laundry line
before wet clothes weigh it down
heavy
making it sag,

she waits
she looks;

Where is the sun,
where is the wind

to lighten the load
before the lines break?

— MIHEE KIM-KORT

We Would Not Have Made It

If it had not been the LORD who was on our
side, when our enemies attacked us,
then they would have swallowed us up alive.

—Psalm 124:2-3

If it had not been the Lord, I would not have made it.

Through accidents that left first responders in awe
    as I walked away without a scratch;
Illness and virus that suddenly, inexplicably
    arrested my breath and threatened my life;
Interaction with trigger-happy police aggressively approaching me in
    stopped vehicles with hands on guns;
Running through MTA cars and up subway steps to avoid predation
    from those trying to assault me;
Hot spots where bullets fly from d-boys' Glocks
    a block over from my bedroom;
Drives with no cell or GPS signal through landscapes flooded with
    confederate flags and white nationalist symbols;
Seasons of poverty marked by potato chip dinners and staying in my
    house because I couldn't afford roundtrip travel on the bus;
Threats of bodily harm from men wanting to roll on me because
    my unapologetic way of being was an irritant to their souls.

Shoutout to God the deliverer! Blessed be their holy name.
If it had not been the Lord who was on my side, on our side,
    we would not have made it.

—ALICIA T. CROSBY

Uncertain

*For the scepter of wickedness shall not rest
on the land allotted to the righteous,
so that the righteous might not stretch out
their hands to do wrong.*

—Psalm 125:3

Who's to say what it means to be righteous?
Who among us gets to say?

Uncertain.

I hold onto this: God is close by, protecting us;
God will not abandon us to the rule of the wicked,
or even to the tempting tools the wicked use.

Or even to the tools that tempt me.

— MARTHA SPONG

You Owe Me More Meaning

*Those who go out weeping bearing the seed for sowing,
shall come home with shouts of joy.*
— Psalm 126:6

I insist that it's true;
I demand it, Creator.
I require that there be meaning;
You owe a better ending than flies on shit.
You do.
"I didn't ask to be born," my son once said;
Actually, he said it a lot.
What say you, Creator?
Your silence is unbearable;
I grieve your absence.
Those who go out weeping
bear the seed for sowing.

I'm coming home, Lord,
with shouts of joy—
see if I don't—
but would it kill you every now and then
to show yourself?

I said to a friend once:
"Thank God I was raped; that trauma made me who I am."
Those who sow in tears reap with shouts of joy;
is this not what you meant?
"What will your therapist say?" my friend asked,
hoping to shake sense into my obstinance,
but I am unshakeable.
You owe me more meaning than flies on shit,

and I will come home
with shouts of joy.
I will turn this curse to blessing;
And if you, too, are abashed
you should be somewhat uncomfortable, God.
I know I am.
If all you can offer is that nothing lasts forever,
then I'll take it;
But hurry up,
because I'm losing my voice.

Praise the Lord,
praise the Lord,
praise the Lord.

— **KATIE MULLIGAN**

Reclaiming My Time

*It is in vain that you rise up early
and go late to rest,
eating the bread of anxious toil;
for he gives sleep to his beloved.*

—Psalm 127:2

In the words of Auntie Maxine, I'm reclaiming my time:

the time I didn't feel the need to do it all,
the time I laughed when I made mistakes,
the time I wasn't afraid to ask for help,
the time I knew what I didn't know,
the time I wasn't crushed by criticism,
the time I didn't fight to stay awake,
the time I fully trusted God.

Yes, I'm reclaiming my time!

— **MARILYN PAGÁN-BANKS**

Flourish the Results

Your wife will be like a fruitful vine within your house;
your children will be like olive shoots around your table.
— Psalm 128:3

What are the rewards for those who fear the Lord but never marry?
Or who have tried to live righteously, but suffer miscarriage?
    What grace is bestowed upon the one who lives a single life?
    Are they forgotten?
Does God look upon them as lesser, as the world so often does?
There is fulfillment without a spouse,
and a whole life can be lived without fruit from the womb.
    What are the stars in the crown of the faithful
    for whom spouse and children are not a reality?
Will their work be honored?
Will their name be remembered?
Will God flourish the results of their labors?

— JULIA SEYMOUR

I Was Not

"Often have they attacked me from my youth,"
—let Israel now say—
"often have they attacked me from my youth,
yet they have not prevailed against me."

—Psalm 129:1-2

My childhood was imperfect, like most,
but I did not fear that walking out of my front door to go to school
    could mean dodging bullets
    or predators
    or any other manner of environmental hazard
    enfleshed in human skin and instability;
My childhood was imperfect, but I was not under attack.
Why (not) me, Lord?

— KENTINA WASHINGTON-LEAPHEART

Sophia

LORD, hear my voice! Let your ears be attentive to the voice of my supplications!
—Psalm 130:2

Sometimes Patriarchy
has me in a choke hold,
a hand over my mouth.
> I struggle against him,
> suffocating, my nose
> clogged with his odor.

Always Sophia
cradles me, her embrace
soothing and strengthening.
> I sink into her arms
> as into the bed
> of my lover.

Sometimes Patriarchy
stands at a distance
his fingers in his ears.
> I shout at him until
> my throat is tattered,
> while he pretends not to listen.

Always Sophia
leans in. Her face alight with
curiosity and compassion.
> I speak, one word or
> a thousand.
> She hearkens. She hears.

Sophia, hear my petition:
remind me that I have the strength

to break free from that which binds—to break that which binds.
    Remind me that I have the voice
        to speak words that bring down and build up
        whenever necessary.

— **JENNIFER GARRISON BROWNELL**

Nursing

But I have calmed and quieted my soul,
like a weaned child with its mother;
my soul is like the weaned child that is with me.
—Psalm 131:2

Late nights,
holding you against my chest
as we slept in a chair together;

you would wake and fuss,
eyes partially closed,

until you found my breast;
you had your fill
and fell silent,
asleep.

I would watch and wait
drinking in your calm,
hoping you would stay like this
for a while.

— MIHEE KIM-KORT

Where God Lives

I will not enter my house
or get into my bed;
I will not give sleep to my eyes
or slumber to my eyelids,
until I find a place for the LORD,
a dwelling-place for the Mighty One of Jacob.

—Psalm 132:3-5

God, I'm tired.

Some days I'm certain I could never leave my bed again.
Some days I drag myself to life like a petulant toddler
kicking and screaming in the middle of a store.

It's not just me. The whole world
has bags under its eyes, laboring to breathe, wincing against its many
      wounds.
a look that says, "I'm not going to make it."

And that's what gets me up, finally: I won't let it die like this.

Keep going, I whisper. You are beautiful and good.
Don't you know you are a holy home?
God dwells here.

— LAYTON E. WILLIAMS

The Taste in My Mouth

How very good and pleasant it is
when kindred dwell together in unity!

—Psalm 133:1

Supposedly we want this, O God,
the sense that all will be well,
that they may all be one;
But I wonder if we think
that love only for the ones most like us will be enough,
as comforting as the buttery spice of cinnamon toast in my mouth.

The flavor of truth
sits sour-milk-acrid on our tongues,
stings our lips like shaving cream pie in the face.

It is the taste of whiteness in my mouth.

—**MARTHA SPONG**

Splay Your Fingers Wide

Lift up your hands to the holy place.

—Psalm 134:2

Lift up your hands, sweet child,
lift them up high.
Stretch to the sky until on your tippy toes
your fingers brush a cloud.
Lift up your hands, sweet child,
like the tallest tree of the forest
seeking sunlight evermore and evermore.

Lift and stretch and grow,
reach as high as you can and then stretch a little more.
Lift and reach and close your eyes in the pleasure of the stretch.
Lift your hands and splay your fingers wide.
Throw your head back and laugh; arch your back and curl your toes.
Hold yourself steady and let out a cry of blessing unto our Creator.

Give thanks for every breath that you take
and every day that is not promised.
Stretch, stretch, stretch, beyond what you dreamt was possible,
and bless the one who made us.
Give thanks for life and possibility and hopes and dreams and maybes.
There will be time enough for grief and rage.
Today, right now, lift your hands and bless the Lord.

— **KATIE MULLIGAN**

Why Did You Choose Violence?

*God it was who struck down the firstborn of Egypt,
both human beings and animals.*

—Psalm 135:8

Holy One, I don't recognize you in this story.
You sent plagues and curses on the enemies of your people,
and then you killed the firstborn in all of Egypt.
If you are God, why did you choose violence?

I don't know what to do with you.
I much prefer you to be
a God of infinite wisdom, compassion, and kindness:
all-loving, if not all-powerful,
all-present, if not all-knowing.

And yet, who am I to question you?
You, Creator of the universe,
Creator of humankind,
Creator of me.
I place my trust in you
and acknowledge that,
in the beginning and in the end,
I am yours.

— **BETH A. RICHARDSON**

136

Gratitude for Their Wonders

O give thanks to the LORD, for he is good,
for his steadfast love endures forever.
—Psalm 136:1

O give thanks to the Lord,
express gratitude for their wonders.
God's genius is unmatched, and their creativity is unparalleled.

Thank you for the sun, O God.
Its warm presence and bright light pierce through
my seasonal affective disorder and help me
rise and produce good works of my own.
Thank you for perspective.
I sit in awe on the edge of the water
looking at the way sky and river or ocean meet
and cry because I see the artistry of your hand.

All of creation is a testament
to the beauty present in your person, God:
early morning bird songs, flowers defiantly pushing through concrete,
the hum of cicadas and crickets,
rolling hills, mighty mountains, and sacred plains,
lakes that go on for what seems like forever.
Remind me of your power and identity as Creative and Creator.

Your affection for me stands out
in the wonders you've brought close
so I can behold their glory and delight in their splendor.

—ALICIA T. CROSBY

Too Far

By the rivers of Babylon—
there we sat down and there we wept when we remembered Zion.
On the willows there we hung up our harps.

—Psalm 137:1-2

Violence drove them from home.
They were spoils of war—enslaved, carried off, exiled.
Sand cut their feet, wind whipped their faces, and always the
    relentless sun beat on.
Their destination was only a rumor:
stately trees lining waterways and bejeweled towers touching the sky,
    it was said.

Upon arrival, they were ripped apart:
spouses separated, children carried off elsewhere, families broken.
In grief and confusion, trapped in this terrible beautiful place, there
    was no music at all.
They did not sing. They could not dance.
Their hope was caught and hung in the branches of the trees.

— JENNIFER GARRISON BROWNELL

My Work

The LORD will fulfill his purpose for me.

—Psalm 138:8

The prophet Dr. Katie Cannon wrote,
    "You must do the work your soul must have."
I believe this so deeply in my heart, yet
    what happens when you're not sure what that work is?

The space between "I am doing what I was put on this earth to do" and
    "WTF am I even doing right now" swallows me whole,
        trapping me in waves of uncertainty and frustration.
The God who so expertly ordered my footsteps and made crooked
    pathways straight
    now seems MIA
while I dodge road hazards of "in the meantime" gigs and
    "way below what I'm worth" salary offers.
Tell me God, how will you fulfill your purpose for me?
    How will you make sense of this?

— KENTINA WASHINGTON-LEAPHEART

I Am All These Things

Where can I go from your spirit?
Or where can I flee from your presence?
If I ascend to heaven, you are there;
if I make my bed in Sheol, you are there.

—Psalm 139:7-8

Hood and holy,
spirit and flesh,
faithful and lost,
strong and weak,
teacher and learner,
shadow and light,
leader and follower
child and grown-ass woman.

I am all these things—
mostly unapologetic,
       sometimes terrified.
God is with me in all my ways, always;
I am never alone.
       Thank you, God!

— **MARILYN PAGÁN-BANKS**

Be a Fence

Guard me, O LORD, from the hands of the wicked;
protect me from the violent who have planned my downfall.
—Psalm 140:4

The anonymous letter offers instruction
    in how to preach "better,"
        to offer messages "our congregation" needs to hear.
Dear to the heart of the letter writer, apparently,
    are messages of condemnation and shame.
They are anathema to me—the voice of Fear disguised as gospel,
    a scraping, hideous sound
        that causes flinching and cringing,
            that imperils those who are most easily dismissed.
Be a fence around me, Lord, protecting me from fear.
Strengthen my hand to file this letter where it belongs.
Let me stand strong against the forces that oppose you
    and build a garden of love with my plowshare,
        a garden that will yield a generous harvest.

—JULIA SEYMOUR

The Good Hurt

Let the righteous strike me;
let the faithful correct me.

—Psalm 141:5a

There is so much I didn't know
when I was young, cozy in my life like a haven.

So much I didn't know of justice and injustice; of real mercy, grace, and love;
of all the violence we do to others to keep our power
and how quickly we betray one another for 30 pieces, just to keep our havens cozy.

I am grateful for the ones who've hit me with the truth.
I give thanks for any painful learning that leads to hurting others less,
for any breaking that breaks up a sinful system and my own faithless complicity.

There was once so much of God and grace I didn't know.
There still is.
God, please keep breaking me open,
so I can let you in.

—LAYTON E. WILLIAMS

Hiding Out

When David was in the cave. A prayer.

—Psalm 142

Well, Lord, I did it again:
tripped up my own damn self;
Yet again I made trouble and then stepped in it.
Had to learn the hard way,
can't seem to pay attention to the lessons elders already learned.
Yet again, here I am, in a cave,
hiding out from people who have good reason to loathe me.
Let me try to do it differently this time—
let me do better be better dream better
Let me have another chance, God. It'll be different this time. No really.

Isn't that always the prayer of the powerful,
and haven't we all prayed it once or twice or ten or a hundred?
No, the prayer from the cave is this:

May you bring healing to those I've caused harm;
May I restore what I can;
May I have the sense
to leave people alone when all I can do is cause pain;
May I find refuge in you and may I use it to change;
May I be satisfied in myself
so that I do not demand from my victims' affirmation;
May you bless me with wisdom and courage and strength
to face who I am
and may that be enough.

— **KATIE MULLIGAN**

Thirst

My soul thirsts for you like a parched land.

—Psalm 143:6

No matter how much I drink
from your wells,

I feel like I'm drowning.

— MIHEE KIM-KORT

Quickly

*May there be no breach in the walls, no exile,
and no cry of distress in our streets.*

—Psalm 144:14

Holy One, the walls have been breached.
Your people are crying,
and we are in exile in our own land.

What is this place in which we live?
Hate marches down city streets at the noon of day.
Abusers walk the halls of justice and power.
Children are stripped from their mothers' arms and sleep in cages.

Holy One, where are you today?
The evildoers hold the fortresses of power.
The exploiters of the poor grow in their wealth.
Your little ones languish in despair.
Calls of distress go ignored in the streets.

Where is our hope?
Where is our rescuer?
Come quickly, God of Compassion
Come quickly to save us.

—BETH A. RICHARDSON

The Glory of Your Kin-dom

They shall speak of the glory of your kingdom, and tell of your power.
—Psalm 145:11

Kin-dom. Family. Assembly of relatives
    who approach the holy of holies boldly
        in varied tongues and postures:
I don't see you as my king but as my God,
my beloved divine parent.
Kings get replaced, and
    imperial function is antithetical
        to the radical love of your justice.
I refuse to speak of a thing that doesn't reflect
who I understand you to be.

Blessed be my Creator:
    the God so devoid of ego that they topple hierarchies and
        cast vision for power that can be shared.
Blessed be the Holy One who hovers over the deep in me
    and calls forth life with me,
        as she did at the dawn of creation.
Blessed be the Ancient of Days whose divine affection
    is present in so many things, but often
        in and through the care of your children.
It is of you and the kin-dom formed in your name that I will speak,
    so long as blood courses through my veins and
        breath occupies my body.

May we grow in love, grow in wisdom, and
grow in grace as we work in unity for your sake;
May the generations commend to one another the family of God;
May it provide resource and refuge for them
in their times of need, forever and ever.

—ALICIA T. CROSBY

Will All Crumble

Do not put your trust in princes, in mortals, in whom
there is no help. When their breath departs, they return
to the earth; on that very day their plans perish.
—Psalm 146:3-4

Okay, listen. Here's what you think I will say.
What you think I will say is something about
    powers and principalities and presidents.

What you think I will say is something like this:
    that the towers of princes,
        even towers with their names spelled out in gold letters,
    will all crumble one day.
What you think I will say is that we can rest,
    satisfied—maybe a little smug even—
    in the sure knowledge that one day
    even the worst despot will be under the ground.

But listen, what I'm going to say is this:
That the first word is not about the powers or principalities or even
    presidents.
The first word is an invitation, a challenge, maybe even a test.
The first word is for you.
The first word is,
    "Hey! You! Yes, you.
    This question is about you, is for you:
    What is your trust?
    And where do you place it?"

— JENNIFER GARRISON BROWNELL

Not True

The LORD lifts up the downtrodden;
God casts the wicked to the ground.

—Psalm 147:6

Not true for Aiyanna Stanley Jones
Not true for Tamir Rice
Not true for Pamela Turner
Not true for Eric Gardner
Not true for Michael Brown
Not true for Sandra Bland
Not true for Trayvon Martin
Not true for Rekia Boyd
Not true for Jemel Robinson
Not true for Oscar Grant
Not true for Mya Hall
Not true for Philando Castile
Not true for Antwon Rose
Not true for Michelle Cusseaux
Not true for Laquan McDonald
Not true for Sheneque Proctor
Not true for Eric Logan
Not true for Jamar Robinson
Not true for Shantel Davis
Not true for Gregory Hill, Jr.
Not true for JaQuavion Slaton
Not true for Miriam Carey
Not true for Brandon Webber
Not true for Ryan Twyman
Not true for Betty Jones
Not true for Quintonio LeGrier
Not true for Kyam Livingston

Not true for Jimmy Atchison
Not true for Willie McCoy
Not true for Tarika Wilson
Not true for Emantic "EJ" Fitzgerald Bradford, Jr.
Not true for DeAndre Ballard
Not true for Tanisha Anderson
Not true for Botham Shem Jean
Not true for Kathryn Johnston
Not true for D'ettrick Griffin
Not true for Robert Lawrence
Not true for Anthony Lamar Smith
Not true for Ramarley Graham
Not true for Megan Hockaday
Not true for Manuel Loggins, Jr.
Not true for Kendra James
Not true for Wendell Allen
Not true for Kendrec McDade
Not true for Alberta Spruill
Not true for Larry Jackson
Not true for Yvette Smith
Not true for Randall "Wes" Kerrick
Not true for Jordan Baker
Not true for Victor White III
Not true for Dontre Hamilton
Not true for Korryn Gaines
Not true for Terrence Sterling
Not true for Joyce Curnell
Not true for John Crawford, III
Not true for Ezell Ford
Not true for Dante Parker
Not true for Eleanor Bumpurs
Not true for Kajieme Powell
Not true for Akai Gurley
Not true for Rumain Brisbon
Not true for Aura Rosser
Not true for Jerame Reid

Not true for Charly Keunang
Not true for Gabriella Nevarez
Not true for Natasha McKenna
Not true for Walter Scott
Not true for Gynnya McMillen
Not true for Freddie Gray
Not true for Brendon Glenn
Not true for Ralkina Jones
Not true for Samuel DuBose
Not true for Sharmel Edwards
Not true for Christian Taylor
Not true for Symone Marshall
Not true for Jamar Clark
Not true for Redel Jones
Not true for Mario Woods
Not true for Kayla Moore
Not true for Danette Daniels
Not true for Shereese Francis
Not true for Gregory Gunn
Not true for Jessica Williams
Not true for Akiel Denkins
Not true for Kisha Michael
Not true for Alton Sterling
Not true for Frankie Ann Perkins
Not true for Nizah Morris
Not true for Kathryn Johnston
Not true for Terence Crutcher
Not true for Alexia Christian
Not true for Keith Lamont Scott
Not true for Sonji Taylor
Not true for Alfred Olango
Not true for India Beaty
Not true for Jordan Edwards
Not true for Stephon Clark
Not true for Malissa Williams
Not true for India Kager

Not true for Danny Ray Thomas
Not true for DeJuan Guillory
Not true for Shelly Frey
Not true for Alesia Thomas
Not true for Patrick Harmon
Not true for Margaret Laverne Mitchell
Not true for Jonathan Hart
Not true for Tyisha Miller
Not true for Maurice Granton
Not true for Janisha Fonville
Not true for Pearlie Golden
Not true for Duanna Johnson
Not true for Latanya Haggerty

— **MARILYN PAGÁN-BANKS**

Get Excited!

Let them praise the name of the LORD,
for he commanded and they were created.

—Psalm 148:5

Let's get excited about God!
You jaguars and grizzly bears, roar to the One who made and keeps you.

Let's dance with divine inspiration!
You dolphins and frogs, leap with joy toward the highest heaven.

Let's sing together a song of salvation!
You wolves and red-tailed hawks, exult in your freedom and
 belovedness.

Let's worship the Spirit who brings order out of chaos.
You sea otters and kangaroos, give thanks with your whole being.

Let's listen to the Love that is the source of all healing.
You pronghorns and pandas, rest in the everlasting arms of provision.

Let's celebrate grace, unearned concession freely and generously given!
You snails and blue whales, embrace your vocations.

Let's praise God as a united creation!
You siblings and friends, you neighbors and strangers, you ascetics and
 revelers,

Let us praise the Lord—eternal Love poured out in, among, and for us.

— JULIA SEYMOUR

Good Music

Praise the LORD! Sing to the LORD a new song.

—Psalm 149:1

Does God tire of our repetitive hymns of old
    or the contemporary songs some call "good music"?
Perhaps God is exhausted of the tone deafness of our melodies,
    the harmonies that are always slightly off-key,
    the out-of-tune compositions,
    the out-of-sync rhythms.
Perhaps God is tired of our flat worship notes
    and pitchy pontifications.
But how can we sing a new song
    when we struggle to forget the words we know?

— KENTINA WASHINGTON-LEAPHEART

Exhale Glory

Let everything that breathes praise the LORD!
—Psalm 150:6a

Start with a breath. Put your hand on your belly.
Do you feel it swelling?
Pull the breath deep and let your voice soar!

Sing sweet, loud, off-key,
velveted or raggedy,
wispy or ferocious.

Breathe in, then exhale glory to the One who made you!
Use the voice God gave you;
find the notes in the church, in the shower, in the car!

You are an instrument of praise!
Breathe, and sing, and praise God!

—MARTHA SPONG

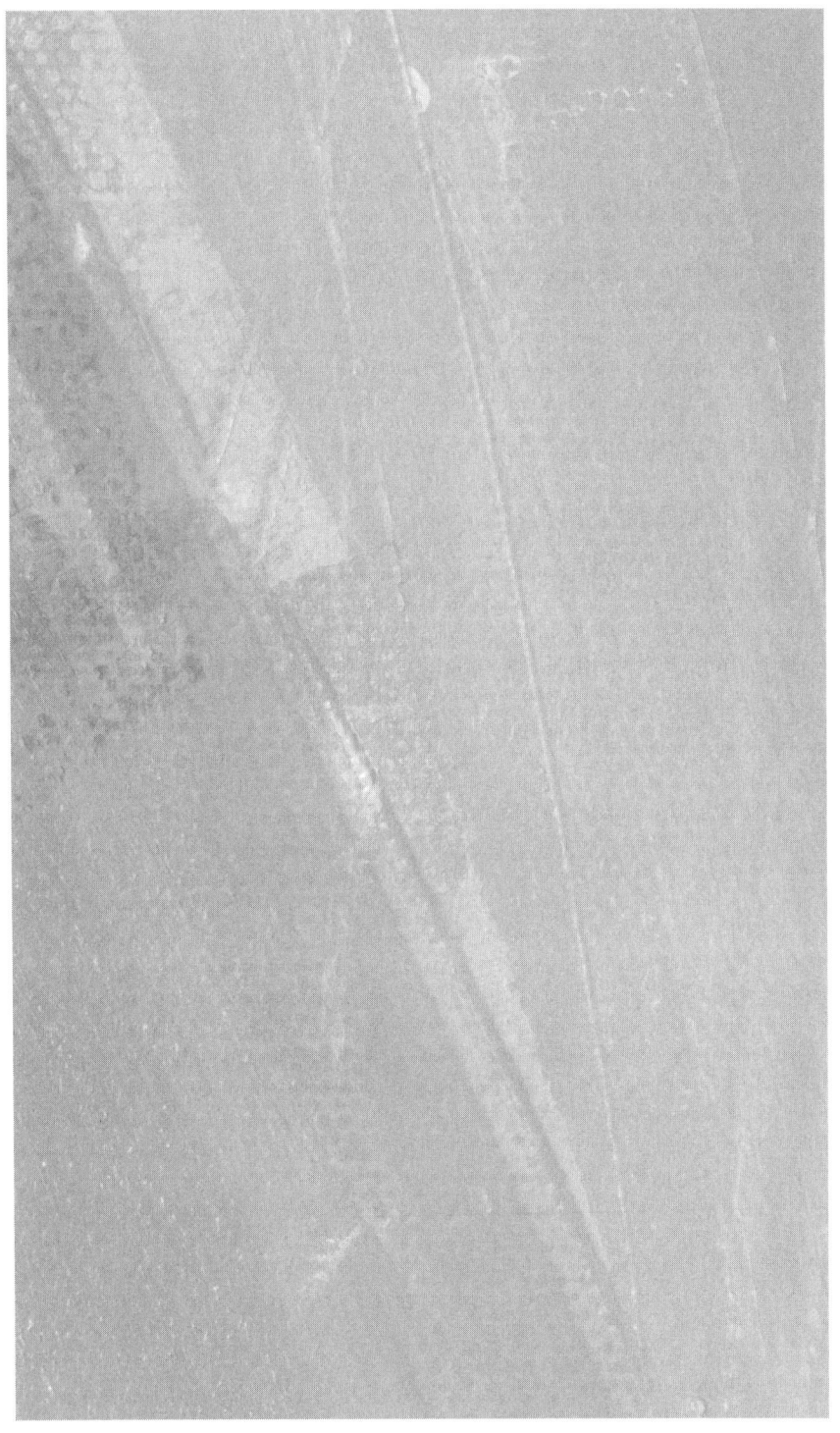

Acknowledgments

As this book comes to birth, I want to thank the nine women who engaged the Psalms with me and brought their full, beautiful selves to the project. I am grateful to Rachel Hackenberg at The Pilgrim Press, both for fleshing out the idea for this book with me, and for her editorial and design eye. And I thank my wife, Kathryn Johnston, for being both colleague and best friend, and for believing in me at every phase of the writing process; I love you all the ways.

— **MARTHA SPONG, EDITOR**

About the Editor

The Rev. Martha Spong is an author, United Church of Christ pastor, and clergy leadership coach committed to sustaining clergywomen in their work and amplifying diverse voices in conversations about faith, particularly People of Color and LGBTQIA+ people. As Executive Director of RevGalBlogPals from 2013 to 2020, she emphasized ecumenical collaboration and created space for reflections on the intersection of faith and public life in a weekly feature, "The Pastoral is Political." Under her leadership, RevGalBlogPals received the United Church of Christ's Antoinette Brown Catalyst Award for providing a provocative space that advances women in ministry. Martha is co-author with Rachel Hackenberg of *Denial is My Spiritual Practice (and Other Failures of Faith)* and the editor of *There's a Woman in the Pulpit: Christian Clergywomen Share Their Hard Days, Holy Moments, and the Healing Power of Humor.* Martha lives in Pennsylvania with her Presbyterian pastor wife and their family.

Contributors

The Rev. Jennifer Garrison Brownell grew up near a big lake in Northern Minnesota and now lives near a big river in the Pacific Northwest. Jennifer is pastor of Vancouver United Church of Christ in Vancouver, Washington, contributor to the book *There's a Woman in the Pulpit: Christian Clergywomen Share Their Hard Days, Holy Moments and the Healing Power of Humor* and the author of the memoir *Swim, Ride, Run, Breathe: How I Lost a Triathlon and Caught My Breath*. She loves yoga, her tall son, her girlfriend's morning prayers, bananas, Jesus, and the useless, adorable animals in her life—not necessarily in that order.

Alicia T. Crosby (she/hers) is a justice educator, activist, and (sometimes reluctant) minister whose work addresses the spiritual, systemic, and interpersonal harm people experience. Through her writing, speaking, and space curation, Alicia helps individuals, communities, and institutions explore and unpack topics related to identity, inclusivity, and intersectional equity. She is currently a student at Duke Divinity School You can follow her work via aliciatcrosby.com or on Facebook, Twitter, and Instagram via @aliciatcrosby.

Mihee Kim-Kort is a Presbyterian minister, agitator, speaker, writer, and slinger of hopeful stories about faith and church. Her writing and commentary can be found at TIME, BBC World Service, *USA Today, Huffington Post, Christian Century,* On Being, Sojourners, and Faith and Leadership. Her most recent work is *Outside the Lines: How Embracing Queerness Will Transform Your Faith*. She is a PhD student in Religious Studies at Indiana University where she and her Presbyterian minister-spouse live with their three kids in Hoosier country.

The Rev. Katie Mulligan is a pastor in the Presbyterian Church (USA) and has served several churches in New Jersey, working with youth and adults and organizing with grass roots community groups around racial justice, LGBTQ concerns, and poverty. Katie was a contributor to *There's a Woman in the Pulpit: Christian Clergywomen Share Their Hard Days, Holy Moments, and the Healing Power of Humor.*

Contributors

The Rev. Dr. Marilyn Pagán-Banks (she/her/hers/ella) is a queer womanist freedom fighter, minister, spiritual entrepreneur, teacher, and lifelong learner committed to the liberation of colonized peoples, building power and creating community. She lives in Chicago with her spouse and has three children and nine grandchildren. Dr. Pagán-Banks currently serves as executive director of A Just Harvest, pastor at San Lucas UCC, and adjunct professor at McCormick Theological Seminary.

The Rev. Beth A. Richardson is an ordained clergyperson and a member of the Mountain Sky Conference of The United Methodist Church. She serves The Upper Room as the Director of Prayer and Worship Life and Dean of the Upper Room Chapel, and is a member of the North American Academy of Liturgy. A native of Oklahoma, she is a photographer, cartoonist, worship nerd, and friend of dogs. Her books include *Christ Before Me, Christ Within Me: Celtic Blessings*; *The Uncluttered Heart: Making Room for God During Advent and Christmas*; *Child of the Light: Walking through Advent and Christmas*; and *Jack's Book of Blessings: Celtic Poems by a Scottie Dog*.

The Rev. Julia Seymour (she/her/hers) is an ordained minister of the Evangelical Lutheran Church in America (ELCA) and she serves Big Timber Lutheran Church in Big Timber, Montana. She was dedicated in an Assembly of God congregation, baptized in a Southern Baptist one, confirmed in a congregation of the Episcopal Church, and was ordained in the Evangelical Lutheran Church in America in 2008. She lives in Montana with her husband, their two children, a dog, and a rabbit. Julia enjoys knitting, reading, gardening, and exploring hot springs and swimming holes. She currently serves as board president for RevGalBlogPals, Inc., an international online community created to support clergywomen and their friends.

Contributors

The Rev. Kentina Washington-Leapheart is a self-identified womanist, queer laborer for the Jesus Project recognized by Garrett Evangelical Theological Seminary's Center for the Church and the Black Experience as one of Garrett's 45 Outstanding Alums. Kentina has combined her love for justice, education, pastoral care, and chaplaincy as a chaplain in hospitals, hospices, and long-term care facilities, and as Director of Programs for Reproductive Justice and Sexuality Education at the Religious Institute. Ordained in The Fellowship of Affirming Ministries (TFAM) by Bishop Yvette Flunder in 2018, Kentina shares her life with her wife, the Rev. Naomi Washington-Leapheart and their daughter, and she considers her relationship with her family and friends as her primary and most important ministry.

The Rev. Layton E. Williams is a writer and an ordained minister in the Presbyterian Church (USA) and the author of *Holy Disunity: How What Separates Us Can Save Us*. She previously served at Fourth Presbyterian Church in Chicago and then on staff at Sojourners in Washington, DC. She currently lives in Charleston, South Carolina, where she serves as Director of New Dawn Ministries at Sunrise Church and seeks to minister in ways that offer understanding, justice, and relationship in the midst of division.